GOD'S WONDERFUL WAYS

a third book of Christian assemblies for schools

Michael Forster

Kevin Mayhew

First published in 1997 by
KEVIN MAYHEW LTD
Rattlesden
Bury St Edmunds
Suffolk IP30 0SZ

ISBN 1 84003 076 3
Catalogue No 1500146

0 1 2 3 4 5 6 7 8 9

Front cover by Jennifer Carter
Edited by David Gatward
Typesetting by Louise Hill
Printed in Great Britain

Contents

Foreword

This is the third in the series of books for school assemblies and, on the principle of 'If it ain't broke, don't fix it', the same basic format has been retained: a story based on the Bible, retold in an imaginative way, sometimes through the eyes of a particular character, forms the basis of each session and is supplemented with material for the class to use in preparing the assembly and to promote discussion and/or learning during it. As before, much additional detail has been added, the important aim being not merely to retell a story but to bring out the essential point of it in ways applicable to today. Each story is retold in a modern colloquial style in order to bring to life the characters and more importantly the issues and principles contained within it. In order to enable as much participation as possible, each story contains some actions for the group to join in and there is an alternative version with speaking parts for several children.

The assumption is that one class or group of children will be preparing an assembly for a larger number, and the hope is that both the preparation and the day itself can involve the children and stimulate their thinking.

A number of songs are suggested for each session. This list is of course very far from exhaustive, and individual teachers and pupils may have better suggestions to make. In the two previous books in the series, songs were taken from a number of sources. However, since then we have seen the publication of *The Children's Hymn Book* (Kevin Mayhew, 1997) and unless otherwise stated all songs recommended here are taken from that book, although many are also available from various other places. The initials 'WUW' after a song refer to *Wake Up, World!* (Kevin Mayhew, 1993).

Once again, much enjoyment has been found in the preparation of this book, and I hope it will be enjoyable and stimulating to use.

MICHAEL FORSTER

Snake in the Grass

Based on Genesis 3

BEFORE THE DAY

Imagine a child has stolen from a supermarket. Get the class to write down how different characters might react, e.g: 'No one told me I shouldn't'. 'I'm his mother, but I can't watch him all the time.' 'I'm the store manager; I have to make the goods look as tempting as possible.' 'I'm the area manager. I set sales targets for the store manager.' 'I'm a customer. I just want cheap food.' Can you think of others?

• Think about the actions for all the children to join in during the story

ON THE DAY

Introduction

We're going to hear a story today about people who blamed each other when things went wrong. First, we'll say our 'Thank you' prayer.

'Thank you' Prayer

Thank you, God, for all you give us,
thank you for the earth and sea;
thank you, God, for special people,
thank you, God, for making me.

God's Story

Cecil the serpent was hiding in some bushes, thinking what a lot of fun he was going to have getting his own back. When God had made the garden, Cecil had thought he was going to be put in charge of it. Then imagine his horror when God created a completely new kind of animal and put *them* in charge. Human beings, they were called. Well, that was a silly name for an animal to begin with, and they were such newcomers! Actually, Cecil hadn't been there all that long either, as it was a new garden, but because he had been around just that bit longer he thought that made him better.

'These new animals!' he thought. 'They come in here and think they own the place!' Then he overheard God talking to the humans.

'Now,' said God, 'you can eat any fruit you find in the garden, except from that tree in the middle.'

'Why?' asked the female human, who was called Eve.

'It's the tree of knowledge,' said God, 'the knowledge right and wrong, and you must not eat from it or you will die.'

Cecil waited a few minutes and squirmed up close to Eve.

'Ooh!' yelled Eve. 'You didn't half frighten me. What do you think you're doing, sneaking up on people like that?'

'Oh,' thought Cecil, 'it's "people" now, is it? Only here five minutes and she thinks she's a whole species.' But he put on his nicest smile and said, 'I'm ssso sssorry to have ssscared you. I'm Sssesssil the ssserpent, and I wanted to sssay welcome to thisss Garden of Eden.'

'Well, that's very kind of you, I'm sure,' said Eve. 'No offence meant.'

'None taken,' said Cecil. 'Have you sssampled sssome of the delicasssiesss around here? Sssome of the fruit is sssimply ssscrumptiousss – essspecially that tree in the sssentre of the garden.'

'Oh,' said Eve, 'God said we mustn't eat from it or we'll die.'

'Why,' said Cecil, 'that'sss sssilly! Sssmall-minded sssensssorship! God doesssn't want you to be wise like him, that'sss all.'

Eve was interested. 'You mean,' she asked, 'that if I eat that I'll be as wise as God?'

'Sssertain as sssunshine in Ssseptember!' answered Cecil. 'Try it – it'sss sssensssational!'

Well, the fruit looked tempting – round, plump, and probably juicy, and Eve thought that to be as wise as God would be wonderful. So:

• she *picked the fruit*
• she *took a bite,*
• and she *licked her lips.* Yum!

Just then her husband Adam came along and really blew his top. 'You haven't eaten that, have you?' he said.

'Of course I have,' said Eve. 'I knew God was only trying to frighten us – here, have some.'

Adam hesitated a moment, and then took the fruit and bit into it. It certainly was lovely. Just as he was enjoying it, Eve shrieked at him so that he nearly swallowed the pips. 'You haven't got any clothes on!'

'What!' exclaimed Adam, and got very embarrassed. Then he looked at Eve and said, 'Neither have you.' Now the silly thing is they'd *never* had any clothes on, but they just hadn't bothered about it until they ate the fruit. But now, for some strange reason, they were rushing round the garden trying to find leaves to cover themselves with. Cecil hadn't had such a good time since he was created. He just laughed and laughed until his sides hurt – and he hadn't got any hands to hold them with!

Then he heard the sound of God's voice: 'Adam, where you?' Adam and Eve were nowhere to be found, but were hiding from God because they were embarrassed. Eventually, God found them and asked, 'What's going on? Have you eaten from that tree?'

'It's not my fault,' babbled Adam. 'The woman made me do it.'

'Oh, that's right,' said God, 'blame the woman for it. After all, you might as well start as you mean to go on!'

Then Eve said, 'Don't blame me – Cecil made me do it.'

'What?' said God, 'Cecil the Serpent? But you're supposed to be better and more intelligent than he is.'

'Huh!' thought Cecil. 'That shows what you know!'

'Well,' said God, 'that's torn it! I hoped you'd all live happily together – people, animals, everything – but you're quarrelling and blaming one another right at the start. Life's obviously going to be difficult, and painful, and people and animals will be fighting one another, all because you couldn't just live together the way I wanted. Well, you can get out of the garden, for a start. Go and work for your livings. And you,' he said to Cecil, 'Since you seem to enjoy saying esses I'll fix it so that that's all you *can* say from now on.'

'Sssssssssss!' said Cecil, partly because he was angry and partly because he couldn't say anything else. He was so embarrassed that he just lay down on his stomach and crawled away. And that's how he's been ever since. Men, women and animals carry on fighting and blaming one another, and nobody ever wants to admit being wrong.

No wonder we make ourselves unhappy!

Our Story

Set the scene, and then get some of the children to read out their work. Are they all *equally* responsible? Are any completely blameless? Does any of this excuse the actual theft? What does taking responsibility mean for these different people?

Prayers

We're Glad

Thank you, God,
for not giving up on us,
even when we give up on you.
Thank you for calling us,
and helping us to accept
our responsibilities.

We're Sad

Please forgive us, God,
when we blame others
for what we have done.
Help us to be more caring,
and more honest.

Let's Pray for People

Loving God,
this is sometimes an unhappy world,
and sometimes people and animals get hurt.
We pray for people who are ill, or in pain;
people who are poor,
people who have no homes.
Help them to know that you haven't given up.
Help us to show them that.

Songs

Everyone says, 'It's not my fault.' (WUW)
Do what you know is right
When God made the garden of creation
When your Father made the world

Snake in the Grass

God's Story

Narrator	Cecil the serpent was hiding in some bushes, listening as God gave Adam and Eve their instructions.
God	Now, you can eat any fruit you find in the garden, except the fruit on that tree in the middle. It's the tree of knowledge, and if you eat from it you will die.
Narrator	Cecil waited a moment and squirmed up close to Eve.
Eve	Ooh! You didn't half frighten me. What do you think you're doing, sneaking up on people like that?
Cecil	*(Aside)* Oh! 'People' now, is it? Only here five minutes and she thinks she's a whole species. *(To Eve)* Sssorry to have ssscared you. I'm Sssesssil the ssserpent.
Eve	Pleased to meet you, I'm sure.
Cecil	Have you sssampled the fruit from that tree in the sssentre of the garden?
Eve	God said we mustn't eat from it or we'll die.
Cecil	Why, that'sss sssilly! Sssmall-minded sssenssssorship! God just doesssn't want you to be wise like him.
Narrator	Well, the fruit looked tempting. So:

- she *picked the fruit*
- she *took a bite*
- and she *licked her lips*. Yum!

Just then her husband Adam came along.

Adam	You haven't eaten that, have you?
Eve	Of course I have. I knew God was only trying to frighten us – here, have some.

Narrator	Just as Adam was enjoying it, Eve shrieked at him.
Eve	You haven't got any clothes on!
Adam	What! *(Pause)* Neither have you.
Narrator	Now the silly thing is they'd *never* had any clothes on, but until they ate the fruit it hadn't mattered. Now, they were rushing round the garden trying to find leaves to cover themselves with.
Cecil	I haven't had this much fun since I was created!
Narrator	Then they heard the sound of God's voice.
God	Adam, have you eaten from that tree?
Adam	It's not my fault. The woman made me do it.
God	Oh, that's right – blame the woman.
Eve	Don't blame me – Cecil made me do it.
God	But you're supposed to be more intelligent than him.
Cecil	*(Aside)* Huh! That shows what you know!
God	Well, that's torn it! Life's obviously going to be difficult, and painful, and people and animals will be fighting one another, all because you couldn't just live together the way I wanted. Well, you can get out of the garden, for a start. Go and work for your livings. And you *(Turning to Cecil)*; since you seem to enjoy saying esses I'll fix it so that that's all you *can* say from now on.
Cecil	Sssssssssss!

God's Incredible Promise

Based on Genesis 12-21

BEFORE THE DAY

Ask the children to write or draw about things they would like to have, or to do when they are older but which are not possible now. Make up a display entitled 'Worth Waiting For'.

• Think about the actions for all the children to join in during the story.

ON THE DAY

Introduction

We're going to hear a story about some people who waited a long time for God to keep his promise. First we'll say our 'Thank you' prayer.

'Thank you' Prayer

Thank you, God, for all you give us,
thank you for the earth and sea;
thank you, God, for special people,
thank you, God, for making me.

God's Story

Abraham and Sarah were quite old, so they were a little bit surprised – well, no, actually they were absolutely flabbergasted – when God said, 'I want you to move to a new place, and I'm going to use you to start off a whole new nation.'

Now, Abraham could have said, 'Children – at our age? Pull the other one, Big G.' But he thought, 'Well, if God says so, who am I to argue?' And he and Sarah packed up all their things and set off. They didn't know where they were going, or what they would find, and they had to leave behind a lot of friends, and all kinds of things they loved.

Abraham and Sarah had some wonderful adventures on the journey – and some pretty terrifying ones as well – but we haven't got all week, so I'm just going to tell you some parts of the story. Abraham went to Egypt, and had a look around, but being a tourist wasn't as easy then as it is now, and he didn't stay all that long. So they carried on moving from place to place, sometimes being baked by the sun, at others being threatened by wild animals and robbers, and all the time a niggling little voice at the backs of their minds kept saying, 'How can God give us children when we're so old? If he doesn't get on with it, he'll be too late.' Most of the time, they believed God but they did have their doubts – it's only natural, really. They even tried to hurry God along a few times and take the occasional short cut, but it didn't work. God knew what he was doing, which was a good thing because Sarah and Abraham sometimes didn't!

After more than twenty years of this, most of us would have been beginning to give up hope, and Abraham, to be honest, was getting a bit doubtful; and then God spoke to him. 'You and I have a special friendship,' said God, 'and because of that I'm going to make a great nation from you. Your part of it is to trust me.'

Abraham actually thought this was quite amusing. 'Me, a father, at a hundred years old?' he said, (actually he was ninety-nine but at that age who's counting?) 'and Sarah's nearly ninety.' But God was quite insistent that they would have a child, and lots and lots of great-grand-children.

Then one day some strangers arrived. Abraham and Sarah didn't know that the men were really angels, but anyway they were good hosts and gave them some food. Abraham sat with the visitors while they were eating out-side the tent, and one of them asked, 'Where's your wife?'

'She's in the tent,' said Abraham. Actually, she was standing in the doorway listening.

'I'll come back next year,' said the man, 'and you can show me your son.'

Sarah laughed at that. 'Me?' she thought. 'Ninety years old, and with a body that's seen better days – don't be daft!'

The man turned to Abraham and said, 'Why did your wife laugh just now?'

'What me?' replied Sarah, from the doorway, 'I didn't laugh – Oh goodness me no! I wouldn't be so rude as that. It must have been a passing bird – the ones round here have a very strange mating call, you know.'

'Oh no', said the man, 'You laughed all right!'

Sarah was embarrassed, and went back into the tent and pretended to be very busy. Then, for a while, she and Abraham forgot about the visitors and the silly conversations, because they had other things to think about.

As the year went on, Abraham said to Sarah, 'You know, I think you're putting on weight.'

'Don't be silly!' said Sarah, but secretly she wondered about it. They were doing a lot of walking, and life was quite hard, but even with all the exercise she kept on getting bigger. Can you imagine what it was?

One day, she said to Abraham, 'I could really do with a date and onion sandwich.'

'A what!' said Abraham.

'A date and onion sandwich,' said Sarah, 'with boiled potatoes and custard for afters.'

Over the next few months, it got worse. Sarah would get up in the middle of the night to raid the larder. When she started eating pomegranates in a mustard-and-mint sauce, Abraham realised what it was.

'You're pregnant!' he said. 'How wonderful!'

At first Sarah didn't believe him, but gradually as time went on she realised that it was true. Eventually, she had a son. It was the talk of the neighbourhood! A beautiful, bonny bouncing boy, whom she and Abraham decided to call Isaac. All the neighbours came to have a look, and the travelling salesmen who passed by on their camels carried the news all over the place. 'Honestly,' they used to say, 'a baby boy – his dad's a hundred years old and his mum's ninety.'

'Well!' said one of their customers, 'I thought your carpets were pricey – but I'm not buying that!' And he roared with laughter.

- He *held his sides*
- he *slapped his thigh*
- and he had to *wipe his eyes*

Sarah and Abraham could hardly believe it, either, but they were wonderfully happy. God had kept his promise.

'It just goes to show,' said Abraham one evening, 'that faith can move mountains.'

Sarah looked up from feeding Isaac. 'Look,' she said, 'I know this is pretty spectacular, but don't go over the top!'

Our Story

Point out the display to the children, and ask why these things have to be waited for: perhaps because they can't be afforded yet, or more probably because the children are not old enough to use them.

Sometimes, God seems to keep us waiting an awfully long time before he keeps his promise.

Prayers

We're Glad

Sometimes, wonderful things happen
just when we least expect them.
Sick people get better,
enemies make friends.
Thank you, God, for knowing best,
and for always being here.

We're Sad

Sometimes, God, we don't trust you enough.
Most times, come to think of it!
We think you've forgotten, or got it wrong.
We're sorry for being impatient.
Please help us to trust you more.

Let's Pray for People

Some people are desperate.
They think nobody cares about them;
they think there's no hope of anything better.
Please, God, help them to learn to trust you.
Help us to show them that we care,
and that *you* care,
and to give them hope.

Songs

Hang on
Peace, perfect peace is the gift
Wait for the Lord

God's Incredible Promise

God's Story

Narrator	Abraham and Sarah were quite old, so they were slightly flabbergasted by what God said to them.
God	I want you to move to a new place, and I'm going to use you to start off a whole new nation.
Abraham	At our age? Oh well, who am I to argue!
Narrator	Abraham and Sarah had some wonderful adventures on the journey, but God's promise still seemed strange.
Sarah	How can God give us children when we're so old?
God	Because you and I have a special friendship, I'm going to make a great nation from you. You just trust me.
Abraham	Could I *really* be a father, at a hundred years old?
Narrator	Actually he was ninety-nine but at that age who cares? Then one day some strangers arrived. Abraham and Sarah didn't know that the men were really angels, but anyway they were good hosts and gave them some food. Abraham sat with the visitors while they were eating outside the tent.
Stranger	Where's your wife?
Abraham	She's in the tent.
Stranger	I'll come back next year, and you can show me your son.
Narrator	Sarah was listening in the doorway. She laughed.
Stranger	Why did your wife laugh just now?
Sarah	What me? I didn't laugh.
Stranger	Oh yes, you laughed all right!

Narrator	A few months later, Sarah said something very odd.
Sarah	I could really do with a date and onion sandwich.
Abraham	A date and onion sandwich?
Sarah	Yes, with boiled potatoes and custard for afters.
Narrator	Over the next few months, it got worse. When Sarah started eating pomegranates in a mustard-and-mint sauce, Abraham realised what it was.
Abraham	You're pregnant! How wonderful!
Narrator	Abraham and Sarah had a beautiful, bonny bouncing boy, whom they called Isaac. All the neighbours came to have a look, and the travelling salesmen who passed by on their camels carried the news all over the place.
Trader	Honestly, his dad's a hundred and his mum's ninety.
Customer	Well! I thought your carpets were pricey – but I'm not buying that!
Narrator	And he roared with laughter.

- He *held his sides*
- he *slapped his thigh*
- and he had to *wipe his eyes*

Narrator	Sarah and Abraham were wonderfully happy.
Abraham	It just goes to show that faith can move mountains.
Sarah	Look, I know this is special, but don't go over the top!

Who Wants a Monarchy?

Based on 1 Samuel 8-10

BEFORE THE DAY

Ask the children to write down or draw things they wish their parents didn't ask them to do: 'I hate washing up'; 'Why should I tidy my room?' etc. Then ask them to draw or write the good things their parents give them: favourite foods, warm clothes, hugs, etc. Then jumble them all up on a display.

• Think about the actions for all the children to join in during the story.

ON THE DAY

Introduction

In a few moments, we'll be hearing about how the Israelites got their first king. Before that, we'll say our 'Thank you' prayer.

'Thank you' Prayer

Thank you, God, for all you give us,
thank you for the earth and sea;
thank you, God, for special people,
thank you, God, for making me.

God's Story

'It's all right for you,' Samuel grumbled. 'Ever since I've been a prophet, people have been moaning at me – they're just never satisfied. Now they've got it into their heads that a king would give them more than I can.'

'Tell me about it!' God replied. 'I've been in this business a lot longer than you have, and it's always been like that. Don't take it personally, though – it's me they're rejecting, not you.'

'I'll tell them you said no, then, shall I?' Samuel asked.

'If you do that, you'll never get any peace,' God replied. 'No, they're adults, so let them choose, but just make sure you tell them what a king will be like, that's all.'

Samuel really wasn't happy. 'Why do I get all the rotten jobs?' he mumbled as he went away to call a public meeting.

'Don't come crying to me,' he said to the people, 'when your sons have been drafted into the army, or into the armaments factories, and your daughters are working in sweatshops. Oh, and you needn't complain when the king steals your best land for his own use, either.'

'We don't care about that,' shouted Ben, a well-known trouble maker, 'we just want a king!'

'Yeah,' added his wife, Sarah, 'we want to be just like all the other nations. They've got kings, so we want one, too.'

'That's typical of you,' Samuel sighed, 'the greatest achievement you can imagine is just to be like everybody else!'

'A king would make everything OK,' said Ben. 'He'd fight all our battles for us, and tell us what to do, and we wouldn't have to think for ourselves any more.'

'Well that should suit you, anyway,' Samuel replied. 'If that's what you want, then you can have your king, but don't say I never warned you.'

Meanwhile, a long way away, a wealthy farmer called Kish was counting his donkeys. 'Oh, bother! Why won't they stand still when I'm trying to count them?' he groaned. 'I'm sure some have got out.'

'Having problems, Dad?' It was Saul, Kish's son; a tall, handsome young man. 'Perhaps I can help?'

'Only if you can find a way of keeping these donkeys still,' Kish grumbled.

Eventually, they managed to count them. 'I knew it!' said Kish. 'There are five donkeys missing. If I had a shekel for every time I've told the men to mend those fences . . . !'

'Don't worry, Dad,' said Saul, 'I'm sure they won't have gone far – why don't you let me go and look for them?'

'I suppose you'd better,' replied his father. 'Just don't you go getting lost as well, though.'

Saul set off, with a few servants, to find the donkeys, but after they had crossed five counties and still not found them, he began to think that they might have strayed a little further than he expected. 'It's no good,' he said to his servant. 'We'd better go home or Dad's going to forget about the donkeys and start worrying about me instead.'

'What about the holy man?' asked the servant.

'Oh, I don't think Dad'll be worrying about him,' Saul answered.

'I mean, why not ask the local prophet if he knows where the donkeys are?' the servant explained. So they set off to find Samuel.

Samuel was just on his way to worship when he saw Saul coming to meet him. 'Now, Samuel,' God said, 'remember what I told you yesterday. This is the man who's going to be king.'

Saul came up to Samuel and said, 'Can you tell me where I can find the local seer?' (That was a name they often used for prophets.)

'I'm a seer,' said Samuel. 'Actually, I'm a pretty good listener, too, but more of that later. Come and have something to eat, and later on I'll tell you what you want to know. Don't worry about those donkeys of yours – they're quite safe. You're going to be the main man around here before long.'

'What, me?' asked Saul. 'But I'm just an ordinary sort of chap, and I come from the least important tribe – why choose me?'

'Never mind that for now,' Samuel answered. 'Time to eat – we've saved the best food for you.'

It was a wonderful meal.

- There was soup to *slurp*
- bananas to *peel*
- and lots of juice to *drink*

After the meal was over, he told Saul, 'God has chosen you to be the first king. You're to look after his people, protect them and help them. Now go home and you'll find that the donkeys you lost are safe, and your father's started worrying about you instead.'

Saul was absolutely amazed at being chosen to be king, but not half so amazed as Ben and Sarah were when Samuel told them.

'What sort of a king is this?' Ben complained. 'We wanted a king that was better than every-body else's – one to put all our enemies in their place – this man's a nobody, from a tiny little tribe no one bothers about.'

Some people are just never satisfied, are they?

Our Story

Look at the display. None of us really likes having to do as we're told, but we all have to (even teachers, ministers and writers!) But being 'the boss' is about more than giving orders; it's about caring as well, and the two are jumbled up together, just like on this display. Sometimes, giving orders is a way of caring (even if it's not always the best one).

Prayers

We're Glad

Thank you, God, for leaders:
for parents, teachers,
and people who make important decisions.
Help us to trust and obey you
most of all.

We're Sad

Sometimes we're like Ben:
never satisfied.
We want other people to take charge,
and then we complain when they do.
Please God, help us always
to be fair to others.

Let's Pray for People

Loving God,
help all people in authority
to be kind and fair,
especially to those
who are in most need.

Songs

Brother, sister, let me serve you
From heaven you came, helpless babe
Jesus' love is very wonderful
Whether you're one

Who Wants a Monarchy?

God's Story

Narrator   Samuel wasn't happy.

Samuel   It's all right for you, God. Ever since I've been a prophet, people moaned at me. Now they're demanding a king.

God   Tell me about it! I've been in this business longer than you have, and it's always been like that. Don't take it personally, though – it's me they're rejecting, not you. All right, give them what they want, but just make sure you tell them what a king will be like, that's all.

Samuel   O great! Why do I get all the rotten jobs?

Narrator   Samuel went away to call a public meeting.

Samuel   Don't come crying to me when your sons have been drafted into the army, and your daughters are working in sweatshops, or when the king steals your best land.

Ben   We don't care about that; we just want a king!

Sarah   Ben's right. We want to be just like all the other nations. They've got kings, so we want one, too.

Samuel   That's typical of you, Sarah! The greatest achievement you can imagine is just to be like everybody else!

Ben   A king would make everything OK. He'd fight all our battles for us, and tell us what to do, and we wouldn't have to think for ourselves any more.

Samuel   Well that should suit you, anyway. All right, you can have your king. But don't say I never warned you.

Narrator   A few days later, on his way to worship, Samuel saw a young man coming to meet him.

God   Now, Samuel, this is the man I want to be king.

Saul	Hello, my name's Saul. Can you tell me where I can find the local prophet?
Samuel	That's me. Come and have something to eat. Don't worry about those lost donkeys your dad sent you to look for – they're quite safe.
Saul	How did you know about those?
Samuel	Trade secret, dear boy. Now to important matters. You'll be the main man around here before long.
Saul	What, me? But I'm just an ordinary sort of chap, and I come from the least important tribe – why choose me?
Samuel	Never mind that for now. Time to eat.
Narrator	It was a wonderful meal.

- There was soup to *slurp*
- bananas to *peel*
- and lots of juice to *drink*

Samuel	God has chosen you to be the first king. You're to look after his people, protect them and help them.
Narrator	Saul was absolutely amazed. So were the Israelites.
Ben	What sort of a king is this? We wanted a king that was better than everybody else's – one to put all our enemies in their place – this man's a nobody, from a tiny little tribe no one bothers about.
Narrator	Some people are just never satisfied, are they?

David Becomes Famous

Based on 1 Samuel 18-19

BEFORE THE DAY

Who are the children's heroes? Get them to collect pictures, newspaper cuttings, etc., of their favourite singers, actors, sports personalities and so on. It's probably advisable not to use anything too valuable, just in case things get mislaid or damaged. Either the day before or the morning of the assembly, enlist the help of the children to put them up on the wall or a board.

• Think about the actions for all the children to join in during the story.

ON THE DAY

Introduction

We're going to hear a story about fame and jealousy in a minute, but first we'll say our 'Thank you' prayer.

'Thank you' Prayer

Thank you, God, for all you give us,
thank you for the earth and sea;
thank you, God, for special people,
thank you, God, for making me.

God's Story

After David had killed Goliath, King Saul was so pleased with him that he asked him to go and live at the palace. Everything seemed to be very good indeed, especially when Saul put David in charge of the army. Now what you have to remember is that there weren't any football clubs or record companies in those days, so if you wanted to be famous you had to do something pretty spectacular. And you hadn't got to be too fussy about what happened to other people, either. David soon made himself very popular by leading the army into battle with the Philistines. He always won, and every time he came back he was a little more famous than when he went away. Crowds of people would line the streets and cheer the army home.

One day, King Saul heard them shouting, 'King Saul has killed thousands, but David has killed tens of thousands!' which only goes to show that people could be as horrible and bloodthirsty then as they can now.

Anyway, Saul was upset. No, that's not true. He was absolutely madly, mind-blastingly furious! 'How can they say that David's a greater soldier than their king?' he thought. 'Just a minute, that's it! They'll be making him king, next. Well, that settles it: he's got to go.'

Next day, Saul wasn't feeling very well – and neither would you be if you'd spent the entire night thinking nasty jealous thoughts about someone else. So (and you can decide for yourself whether you think this was a good idea) David played the harp to him to try and cheer him up. The upshot of that was that Saul threw a spear at him (but since Saul was already in a bad mood it might not have been any reflection on David's playing). David dodged aside, and the spear made a terrible gash in the wall just behind where his head had been.

From then on, Saul kept on thinking of ways to get David killed. When he realised that his daughter Michal (no, not *that* Princess Michael) was in love with David, he thought he saw his chance. 'You can marry her if you like,' he said to David, 'just as soon as you've killed another hundred Philistines.' At the same time, he was thinking, 'With a bit of luck, they'll kill him before he gets to a hundred.'

That plan didn't work, either. Saul had obviously forgotten David was even more lethal with a sword than he was with a harp, and before long not one but two hundred Philistines had bitten the dust and David was being fitted for his wedding suit. Michal was thrilled, because she loved David very much and didn't realise what had been in her father's mind. As far as she was concerned, they would marry, have ten-point-four children (people had bigger families in those days) and live happily ever after.

Meanwhile, David was winning more and more battles, and the people were shouting and screaming every time he appeared in public, while Saul could probably have walked down the street stark naked and not been noticed. So Saul decided it was time to get back to basics and use some good old-fashioned direct action. Yes, that's right: another spear, another gash in the wall, and David still alive to tell the tale – if a little breathlessly – to his wife.

'You're going to have to get away and hide,' said Michal, 'before that father of mine gets seriously businesslike. No, not that way, they're bound to be watching the door – anyone can tell you never went to the military academy.' She got a large laundry basket and a long rope. 'Get in, and I'll lower you down to the ground. They won't be expecting that. Now, have you got a clean hanky? And don't forget to wash your clothes regularly and clean your teeth three times a day.'

Michal had hardly finished lowering David out of the window when she heard a loud knocking, and a voice. 'Open the raid, this is a door. No, that's not right. Oh, you know what I mean.'

Michal looked around quickly and found a life-size statue of one of the family. Well, they didn't have cameras in those days, so it was the next best thing to a photograph. Meanwhile, the person outside the door was getting impatient.

- He *rattled the handle*
- he *peered through the keyhole*
- then he *hammered on the door violently*

'If you don't open this door, I'll – I'll – I'll get very cross.'

Michal covered up the statue with a blanket, and rubbed her eyes to make it look as though she had been crying.

'I'll huff, and I'll puff, and I'll – no, that won't work. I'll think of something, don't you worry,' the voice went on, outside the door.

'You could always turn the handle,' called Michal.

'Oh, yes. What a good idea!' The door opened and in came the captain of the guard. 'The King wants your husband. Pronto.'

'I'm sorry, but he's ill,' Michal sniffed. 'Look, there he is in bed. I'm ever so worried.'

Meanwhile, David went to see his old friend Samuel the prophet and told him the whole story.

'Don't you worry, Davey, boy,' exclaimed Samuel. 'My friends and I are more than a match for Saul. He might be a great warrior, but a crowd of charismatic prophets in full flow is too much even for him!'

And he was right. David was quite safe.

Our Story

Point out the display of famous people. Perhaps the larger group can name others, as well. Do they ever feel jealous? When they do, does it make them feel good, or bad like Saul? So what is the best response to other people's success?

Prayers

We're Glad

Thank you, God,
for all the good or clever
things we can do,
and all the special talents
other people have, too.

We're Sad

We're sorry, God,
for all the times we get jealous
and hurt other people,
Just because they seem more clever
or more popular.
Teach us to work together
to improve your world.

Let's Pray for People

Loving God,
we pray for all people who feel threatened
by someone else's skills.
Help them to be confident
that what they can do
is just as important to you.

Songs

Do you ever wish you could fly
Goliath was big and Goliath was strong
   (*Biggest isn't always best*)
A new commandment
I'm black, I'm white

David Becomes Famous

God's Story

Narrator   After David had killed Goliath, King Saul put him in charge of the army. Every time David won a battle, he was a little more famous than before. One day, King Saul heard the crowd shouting, 'King Saul has killed thousands, but David has killed tens of thousands!' Saul was upset. No, that's not true. He was absolutely furious!

Saul   How can they say that David's a greater soldier than their king? Just a minute, that's it! They'll be making him king, next. Well, that settles it: he's got to go.

Narrator   Next day, Saul wasn't feeling very well. So (and you can decide for yourself whether you think this was a good idea) David played the harp to try and cheer him up. Saul threw a spear at him, but since Saul was already in a bad mood it might not have been any reflection on David's playing. David dodged aside, and the spear made a terrible gash in the wall just behind him. From then on, Saul kept on thinking of ways to get David killed. When he realised that his daughter Michal was in love with David, he had an idea.

Saul   You can marry her if you like, David, just as soon as you've killed another hundred Philistines. *(Aside)* With a bit of luck, they'll kill him first.

Narrator   That plan didn't work, either, and before long David was being fitted for his wedding suit. David kept on getting even more popular. So Saul decided it was time to get back to basics and use some good old-fashioned direct action. Yes, that's right: another spear, another gash in the wall, and David still alive to tell the tale.

Michal   You're going to have to get away, before that father of mine gets seriously businesslike. Get in the laundry basket, and I'll lower you down to the ground. Now,

	have you got a clean hanky? And don't forget to wash your clothes regularly and clean your teeth properly.
Narrator	Soon, the captain of the guard knocked on the door.
Captain	Open the raid, this is a door. No, that's not right. Oh, you know what I mean.
Narrator	Michal looked around quickly and found a life-size statue of one of the family, and put it in the bed. Meanwhile, the captain was getting impatient.

- He *rattled the handle*
- he *peered through the keyhole*
- then he *hammered on the door violently*

Captain	If you don't open this door, I'll – I'll – get very cross.
Narrator	Michal covered up the statue with a blanket, and rubbed her eyes to pretend she had been crying.
Captain	I'll huff, and I'll puff, and I'll – Oh, it's not locked. Now: the King wants your husband. Pronto.
Michal	I'm sorry, but he's ill. Look, there he is in bed.
Narrator	Meanwhile, David went to see his old friend Samuel the prophet and told him the whole story.
Samuel	Don't you worry, Davey, boy, my friends and I are more than a match for Saul. He might be a great warrior, but a crowd of charismatic prophets in full flow is too much even for him!
Narrator	And he was right. David was quite safe.

Choose Your Weapons

Based on 1 Samuel 25:1-35

BEFORE THE DAY

Get the children to ask their parents for any old locks (e.g. padlocks), or lockable items (e.g. trinket boxes, five-year diaries, etc.) which they could bring to school with the keys. It might be advisable to mark the keys with some kind of code to avoid embarrassment later!

• Think about the actions for all the children to join in during the story.

ON THE DAY

Introduction

Soon we're going to hear the story of a very wise woman. But first, we'll say our 'Thank you' prayer.

'Thank you' Prayer

Thank you, God, for all you give us,
thank you for the earth and sea;
thank you, God, for special people,
thank you, God, for making me.

God's Story

David was in real trouble. Everyone knew that he was a better soldier than King Saul, and most of them said so – which tended to make Saul jealous. He was worried that David might be more popular than he was – and no politician likes to come second. Saul used to get terrible depressions and David, who was a bit of a song writer, used to go and sing to him to cheer him up. The trouble was, though, that that just made Saul feel worse, because he knew singers are *always* more popular than politicians. So before long David had to run away or Saul would have killed him.

David took a few friends – well, rather a lot actually – and went to live out in the fields and caves, hiding from Saul. It wasn't difficult to hide since no one liked Saul anyway and people were very willing to help David – especially if he sang them his latest release.

In one place where they were staying, David's men got friendly with some shepherds who worked for a man called Nabal. When they were getting low on food, David thought, 'I know, I'll ask Nabal for help.' He sent a message asking if Nabal could perhaps spare a little food.

Now the name 'Nabal' meant 'churlish', and he was! 'Why can't these fugitives earn their own keep, and not keep sponging off decent people?' he said crossly to his wife.

'Oh, don't be unfair,' said Abigail, who was really much too nice to be married to an old grouch like Nabal. 'David and his men have been really helpful – and they could have just taken what they wanted without asking because they're all trained fighters.'

'Shut up, woman!' said Nabal. 'This is men's talk!' And he sent David's men back with a great big 'No!' (Actually, he used a few more words as well, but 'No' will do for us.)

David was furious. In some ways, he and Nabal were alike: they both thought you could solve a problem by bashing someone! He buckled on his sword, and called his men.

'Four hundred of you come with me,' he said. 'The other two hundred had better guard the camp.' Then they rode out, whooping and yelling, to teach Nabal a lesson.

Abigail was very angry. 'You stupid, pig-headed, half-witted moron!' she screamed at Nabal. 'You wouldn't know a friend if one stood up and bit you, would you! All this time, David and his men have been around, and have you ever lost a single sheep? No. Have you ever had one tiny complaint from anybody? No. But I'll tell you what you have had, you long-eared son of a crossbred donkey: you've had complete security, that's what you've had. No one would dare rob you while David's men are here. And the first time he asks you for anything, what do you do? Just saying "No" isn't enough for you is it? You have to insult him, wind him up, give him reason to hate you. And any time now you're going to have hundreds of heavily armed and very angry freedom fighters showing you what a stupid pig you are! No, sorry – that's unfair – our pigs are relatively intelligent.'

Nabal just sat there and sulked – because that's what his name said.

Abigail stormed out. 'Don't just stand there,' she yelled at the farm hands. 'Go and pack. I want meat, grain, fruit, honey, and a few kegs of wine wouldn't come amiss – enough for an army!' Then she saddled up a donkey – not Nabal, a brainy one – and went out to meet David with the servants following behind with all the presents.

How would she stop David?

- Would she *use her fists*?
- Would she *hold him up at gunpoint*?
- Would she *throw presents at him*?

When Abigail saw David's army coming, she got off her donkey and waved at them to stop. Abigail was very beautiful and she knew that no man was going to ignore her if she seemed to be upset. So when they had stopped, she went over to David and lay down at his feet. 'I'm sorry, my Lord,' she said, 'Please forgive me.'

Now if there were two things David liked they were power and women, and here was a beautiful woman making him feel powerful. So of course David fell for it straight away.

'I'm sorry about my husband,' Abigail sniffed. 'He really lives down to his name, that one! Look, I've brought you lots of food and drink, and I want you to know how grateful I am for the way you've looked after my shepherds. You will forgive me, won't you?'

David smiled at Abigail and said, 'Thank God you came to meet me today! It would have been terrible if we'd done anything to upset you – even though that husband of yours certainly deserves it.'

'Oh he does, my Lord, he does!' agreed Abigail, smiling at David and trying to look as fragile as possible. 'But I'd be so unhappy if you were angry.'

'I'm not angry any more,' said David. 'Thank you for your presents. I'm glad we managed to settle this without using weapons.'

'Without weapons?' replied Abigail with a mysterious smile. 'I'm not so sure about that.'

Our Story

Let some of the children come to the front and try to unlock the various items, trying different keys until they find the right ones. Watch carefully that none of them is tempted to use unorthodox methods! When some of the keys have been identified and locks opened, point out how easy it was once the key had been found. Some people deal with problems in life the way David and Nabal tried to: by 'brute force and ignorance'. Abigail knew that to every problem there's a key and all she had to do was find the right one.

Prayers

We're Glad

Thank you, God,
for people like Abigail.
Thank you for peacemakers,
who care more about others
than they do about themselves.
Help us to find ways of being
peacemakers, too.

We're Sad

We're sorry, God,
for all the times we've been
too proud to say, 'I'm sorry'!
Sometimes we're so proud
that people get hurt.
Help us to be more like Abigail,
and to make peace possible.

Let's Pray for People

We pray for politicians and judges,
for police men and women,
for parents and children.
Help us all to find the key
to open the way to peace.

Songs

And everyone beneath the vine
I come like a beggar
Make me a channel of your peace
I'm black, I'm white, I'm short, I'm tall
Peace, perfect peace is the gift
Peace is flowing

Choose Your Weapons

God's Story

Narrator   David and his friends were on the run, hiding from King Saul, and they were getting low on food.

David   Let's ask that farmer Nabal. I'm sure he'll help us.

Narrator   Now the name 'Nabal' meant 'churlish', and he was!

Nabal   No. Go and earn your living like everybody else.

Narrator   Now, Nabal's wife, Abigail, was really much too nice to be married to an old grouch like him.

Abigail   Why not help? David's men have been really kind to us – and they could have just taken what they wanted without asking because they're all trained fighters.

Nabal   Shut up, woman! This is men's talk!

Narrator   David was furious when he got the message. In some ways, he and Nabal were alike: they both thought you could solve a problem by bashing someone!

David   Come on, men: let's teach Nabal a lesson.

Narrator   Meanwhile, Abigail was very angry with Nabal.

Abigail   You stupid, pig-headed, half-witted moron! All this time, David and his men have been around, and have you had any trouble? No. But I'll tell you what you have had, you long-eared son of a crossbred donkey: you've had complete security. No one would dare rob you while David's men are here. And the first time he asks you for anything, what do you do? Just saying 'No' isn't enough for you is it? You have to insult him. And any time now you're going to have hundreds of heavily armed and very angry freedom fighters showing you what a stupid pig you are! No, sorry – that's unfair – our pigs are relatively intelligent.

Narrator   Abigail packed up some meat, grain, fruit, honey, and a few kegs of wine, then she saddled up a donkey – not Nabal, a brainy one – and went out to meet David.

How would she stop David?

- Would she *use her fists*?
- Would she *hold him up at gunpoint*?
- Would she *throw presents at him*?

Narrator   Abigail was very beautiful and she knew that no man was going to ignore her if she seemed to be upset. David stopped.

Abigail   I'm sorry, my Lord. Please forgive me.

Narrator   Now if there were two things David liked they were power and women, so of course he fell for it.

Abigail   I'm sorry about my husband. He really lives down to his name, that one! Look, I've brought you lots of presents. You will forgive me, won't you?

David   Thank God you came to meet me today! It would have been terrible if we'd done anything to upset you – even though that husband of yours certainly deserves it.

Abigail   Oh he does, my Lord, he does! But I'd be *so unhappy* if you were angry.

David   I'm not angry any more. Thank you for your presents. I'm glad we managed to settle this without weapons.

Abigail   Without weapons? I'm not so sure about that.

A Right Royal Murder

Based on 2 Samuel 11

BEFORE THE DAY

Ask the children to bring in newspaper cuttings, or perhaps write their own words, about events where vulnerable people came off worst. It could be strong people mugging weak people; perhaps cases of school bullying, or rich people getting big pay rises or preferential treatment. Try also to find examples of the proper use of power. For example, the school crossing patrol who stops the cars to let children cross safely. Use your own imagination and local knowledge to help them make up a display of cuttings.

• Think about the actions for all the children to join in during the story.

ON THE DAY

Introduction

We're going to think about power today, and hear about somebody who misused it very badly. First, we'll say our 'Thank you' Prayer.

'Thank you' Prayer

Thank you, God, for all you give us,
thank you for the earth and sea;
thank you, God, for special people,
thank you, God, for making me.

God's Story

King David could be a very bad man when he set his mind to it. Now you may be surprised at that, because we always think of him as a good king – the one specially chosen by God. But then, even the best people can do bad things at times, and even God's chosen people get things wrong. After all, no one's infallible! What was it that David did? Well, it all began when he went for a walk on his rooftop one day. Now let's say right at the start that that's not something which is generally a good idea, but David had a palace with a flat roof and a safety rail round it, so it was safe. Anyway, he was walking around on the roof, looking at the scenery, when he noticed something he thought was rather exciting. He could see right in through the window of a nearby house where a woman was taking a bath. He should have turned away, of course; peeping through people's windows is a bad thing to do – even if you are the king, or the government or whatever – but she really was a very beautiful woman, and David thought, 'Well, it can't do any harm to have a look, can it?' But it could.

As David stood and watched her, he thought to himself, 'She really is a lovely woman.' Then he got fed up with just looking, and decided it was time for action. He went down to his palace and got a servant to find out who she was. Her name was Bathsheba, he was told, and she was married to a man called Uriah who was away in the army. 'What a shame!' thought David. 'Why are all the best ones married?' Anyway, the more he thought about her, the more he wanted to know her. Then he started making silly excuses to himself, like, 'I'm the king – so I can have whatever I want,' and, 'I bet she knew I could see her – she *wanted* me to see her.' And after a little while he had convinced himself that whatever he wanted to do was right. But it wasn't.

'I'll just invite her round for dinner,' he thought. 'There's no harm in that.' But there was.

Gradually, he started seeing Bathsheba more and more often, and then he realised that he was in love with her. He'd like to have her for his wife, but she was married already, and although men could have lots of wives in those days, women could only have one husband. So David knew that, even though he was the king, he couldn't marry Bathsheba.

While David was thinking about this, Bathsheba came to see him. 'I've got some news for you,' she said, 'and I think you'd better sit down before I tell you.'

'Don't be ridiculous, my little bath-cube,' said David. (When people are in love they sometimes call each other silly names, but if children do it they tell you not to be childish – had you noticed?)

'Just tell me the news,' said David.

'I'm pregnant,' said Bathsheba.

David sat down.

'H-h-how did that happen?' he stammered.

Bathsheba gave him a very funny look. 'The question is,' she said, 'what are we going to do about it?'

David knew that he had to do something – and quickly! If Uriah found out, then, king or no king, David would be in trouble.

David had a choice:

- He could do the right thing *(Thumbs up)*
- He could do wrong *(Thumbs down)*
- But he couldn't do both *(Alternate)*
- Which would he do? *(Thumbs down)*

David made a horrible plan. Uriah was in the army, and was away at the war. Now of course, since Uriah was a brave man and a good fighter it would be natural to put him in the most dangerous place, wouldn't it? And if he should then get killed in battle, well, that wouldn't be the king's fault would it? It was just one of the risks of war, wasn't it? And then David could marry Bathsheba. So before long, David had formed a plan and convinced himself that it was perfectly all right for him to carry it out. But it wasn't.

David sent a message to his general at the battlefield, and marked it 'Top Secret'. In those days, that meant that nobody else would find out about it. 'When the next battle starts,' the message said, 'put Uriah right at the front and make sure he gets killed.' Sure enough, a few days later, another message came back from the general, saying, 'Uriah has been killed in battle.'

When she heard the news about her husband, Bathsheba went into mourning. She was very sad and wore black for quite a long time. Then, after a while, she married King David and moved into the palace with him.

David had committed murder. He was a very powerful man, and he had misused his power to get what he wanted. No one would ever know, though – or so he thought. After all, people often got killed in battle, and the only person who knew the truth was the general – who certainly wouldn't say anything if he knew what was good for him. Of course, ordinary people couldn't do that kind of thing. If they did, David would punish them. But David wasn't an ordinary person; he was the king, and he thought that he was above the law. But he wasn't.

For a while, David was very happy. He'd given Uriah a proper military funeral, with a guard of honour, and said how brave he was and what a shame it was he'd been killed, and everybody had cried a lot. So he thought that made everything all right. But it didn't.

David and Bathsheba were very happy together, and for a little while David thought he had got away with it. But he hadn't.

Our Story

Draw attention to the display. All of us have some kind of power: for example over pets or tiny wild creatures. What kind of powerful people do we want to be?

Prayers

We're Glad

Thank you God,
for all those people who *are* honest,
and who don't try to use their position
to hurt others
or to grab what they want.
Thank you, as well
for all who stand up for what is right.

We're Sad

We're sorry, God,
for the times we've tried
to force our own wishes on others.
Please help us to be more loving
especially to people who are easily hurt.

Let's Pray for People

We pray for people who get bullied,
for poor people who get pushed out,
for people who have had precious things,
or people, stolen from them.
Help them to know that you love them,
that they matter to you.

Songs

All of the creatures God had made
Do what you know is right
There are people who live in mansions
When God made the garden of creation

A Right Royal Murder

God's Story

Narrator	King David was a good king – the one specially chosen by God. But then, even the best people can do bad things at times, and even God's chosen people get things wrong. After all, no one's infallible! It all began when David found that from his palace he could see right in through the window of a nearby house where a woman was taking a bath. He should have turned away, of course; peeping through people's windows is a bad thing to do – even if you are the king, or the government or whatever – but she really was a very beautiful woman.
David	Well, it can't do any harm to have a look, can it?
Narrator	But it could. Next, David sent a servant to find out who she was. Her name was Bathsheba, he was told, and she was married to a man called Uriah who was away in the army.
David	Why are all the best ones married? Still, I'm the King – so I can have whatever I want. I bet she knew I could see her – she *wanted* me to see her.
Narrator	David soon convinced himself that whatever he wanted to do was right. But it wasn't.
David	I'll just invite her round for dinner. There's no harm in that.
Narrator	But there was. Things got very serious between them. One day, Bathsheba arrived with some news.
Bathsheba	I'm pregnant.
David	H-h-how did that happen?
Bathsheba	The question is, what are we going to do about it?
Narrator	David had a choice:

- He could do the right thing *(Thumbs up)*
- He could do wrong *(Thumbs down)*
- But he couldn't do both *(Alternate)*
- Which would he do? *(Thumbs down)*

David sent a message to his general at the battlefield, and marked it 'Top Secret'. In those days, that meant that nobody else would find out about it.

David When the next battle starts, put Uriah right at the front and make sure he gets killed.

Narrator And that's exactly what happened. Uriah was killed in battle. Bathsheba went into mourning. Then, after a while, she married King David and moved into the palace with him. David had committed murder. He was a very powerful man, and he had misused his power to get what he wanted.

David No one will ever know. After all, people often get killed in battle. Of course, ordinary people mustn't do that kind of thing, or I would punish them. But I'm the king, and I'm above the law.

Narrator But he wasn't. David gave Uriah a proper military funeral, with a guard of honour, and said how brave he was and what a shame it was he'd been killed, and everybody cried a lot. So he thought that made it all right. But it didn't.

David and Bathsheba were very happy together, and for a little while David thought he had got away with it. But he hadn't.

A Right Royal Telling Off

Based on 2 Samuel 12:1-10

BEFORE THE DAY

Make a list of names of people famous for standing up against bullies in power. Obvious examples might be: Martin Luther King, Jr, Nelson Mandela, Corrie Ten Boom, Oscar Romero, Desmond Tutu. Perhaps you can think of more. Alternatively, gather information about recent famous miscarriages of justice, and the 'ordinary' people who campaigned and fought against them. Get the children to research them and produce potted biographies/histories which can be put on a display.

• Think about the actions for all the children to join in during the story.

ON THE DAY

Introduction

We're going to hear a story about King David in a moment. He thought that just because he was king he could do as he liked, but God had other ideas. First, we'll say our 'Thank you' Prayer.

'Thank you' Prayer

Thank you, God, for all you give us,
thank you for the earth and sea;
thank you, God, for special people,
thank you, God, for making me.

God's Story

Nathan the prophet was sitting in the shade of a tree, enjoying a nap and dreaming about his dinner, when God spoke to him. God's like that. Just when you think you've got a bit of time to spare and you can relax for a few minutes, God goes and speaks to you.

'Have you heard what King David's done?' he asked.

'I've heard some rumours,' said Nathan.

'Well, they're true,' said God. 'David had an affair with Bathsheba, Uriah's wife, and had Uriah killed so that he could marry her. David thinks he's got away with it and I want him to find out that he hasn't.'

'Oh-oh!' said Nathan, anxiously. 'Why do I get the feeling that I'm about to be landed with a nasty job?'

'Probably because you are,' said God. 'Just go and see David and tell him that he's done wrong and he's going to suffer for it.'

'Oh, sure!' answered Nathan. 'I can just see myself going up to the king and telling him that. You know who'll be the next person to get murdered, don't you!'

'Oh come on, Nathan, use your loaf!' said God. 'If you play your cards right, you can have the king on your side before he realises what you're talking about. Have a think about it. Take your time. I'll give you ten minutes.'

'Gee, thanks!' said Nathan. Then suddenly an idea came to him, and he set off to see King David.

'I'm sorry to disturb you, Your Majesty,' said Nathan, 'but there's something I think you should know about.'

'That's all right, Nathan,' said David. 'What's the matter?'

'It's about a rich landowner and his poor neighbour,' Nathan began. 'The rich man has lots of sheep, and his neighbour had just one lamb of his own. He loved it, and he cared for it, and it was like a friend to him.'

'That's nice,' said David, who could be quite sentimental at times. 'Everyone should have a pet.'

'Quite so, Your Majesty,' said Nathan, 'and this little lamb was the only joy in the poor man's life.'

'Why do you keep on saying "was"?' asked David. 'Has something happened?'

'Funny you should ask,' answered Nathan. 'It's that rich neighbour. He had a visitor one evening, and wanted to give him something nice to eat. Now he'd got lots of animals, but he wasn't satisfied with that. So do you know what he did?'

David was beginning to guess, and he was getting angry.

Nathan went on. 'He stole his neighbour's

little lamb,' he said, 'and left him with nothing at all.'

David was furious. He hated injustice, and he loathed bullies. 'That's outrageous!' he shouted. 'Just because he's rich, that doesn't mean he can do as he likes. I'll make him pay for it! In fact, I'll make him pay several times over! I'll make his life a misery! I'll make him wish he'd never been born!'

David was getting more and more worked up. He strode about the room, banging his fist into his other hand, and knocking over tables, and his shouting got louder and louder until the neighbours were wondering what had happened. Then he turned to Nathan, and looked at him through angry eyes. 'Tell me who he is!' he roared. 'Tell me who he is, and I'll see he gets everything he deserves.'

'It's you,' said Nathan.

'Right!' yelled David. 'Call out the guard! Send for the executioner! I won't tolerate this kind of . . .'

David was amazed!

- He *blinked in astonishment*,
- he *scratched his head*,
- and then he *put his face in his hands*

David stopped and went very quiet. After a few moments, he said, 'What did you say?'

'It's you,' Nathan repeated. 'You've got a palace full of beautiful women. Uriah had just one wife, and he loved her. But you wanted her, and just because you're the king you thought you could take her.'

David realised then what a terrible thing he had done, and he listened very quietly as Nathan went on talking.

'A corrupt king is a bad king,' said Nathan. 'You can't expect people to love you and respect you when you behave like this. I'm afraid you're going to have a lot of trouble with your people and with your own family. You're in for a very bad time indeed.'

'I deserve it,' said David, who really was very sorry for what he had done.

'And you'll be even sorrier,' said Nathan.

Soon after that, the baby of David and Bathsheba became ill. David was terrified that the child might die, and he stopped eating and spent every day praying. It was no good, though. After a few days the child died. David and Bathsheba tried to comfort one another. 'We can't change the past,' said David, 'that's gone. But perhaps we can change the future. I'm going to be a better king, and that means being a better person.'

David became a great king, and soon he and Bathsheba had another baby – a very special one – and they named him Solomon

Our Story

Show the group the display and invite some of the children who helped create it to say what it means to them.

Prayers

We're Glad

Thank you, God, for friends,
especially the real ones,
who are honest with us.
Thank you for using them
to help us see ourselves more clearly.
And thank you for loving us
even when we don't deserve it.

We're Sad

We're sorry, God,
for the double standards we live by,
when we hurt other people
to get what we want.
Help us to be honest with ourselves.

Let's Pray for People

We pray for victims of crime,
and for all who live in fear of it.
Please God, help the people who commit it
to see it from the victims' point of view.

Songs

Goliath was big and Goliath was strong
He was born in the winter
He's got the whole world in his hands
Make me a channel of your peace

A Right Royal Telling Off

God's Story

Narrator Nathan the prophet was enjoying a nap and dreaming about his dinner when God interrupted him. God's like that. Just when you think you can relax for a few minutes, God goes and speaks to you.

God Have you heard what King David's done? He had an affair with Uriah's wife, and had Uriah killed so that he could marry her. He thinks he's got away with it.

Nathan Oh-oh! Why do I get the feeling that I'm about to get landed with a nasty job?

God Probably because you are. Just go and tell David that he's done wrong and he's going to suffer for it.

Nathan Oh, sure! You know who'll be the next person to get murdered, don't you!

God Use your loaf, Nathan! If you play your cards right, you can have the king on your side before he realises what you're talking about. Have a think about it. Take your time. I'll give you ten minutes.

Nathan Gee, thanks!

Narrator Suddenly Nathan had an idea, and went to see the king.

David What can I do for you, Nathan?

Nathan It's about a rich landowner and his poor neighbour. The rich man has lots of sheep, and his neighbour had just one lamb that he loved and cared for.

David That's nice. Everyone should have a pet.

Nathan Quite so, Your Majesty. But one evening, the rich neighbour had a visitor and wanted to give him something nice to eat. Now he'd got lots of animals, but he wasn't satisfied with that. So do you know what he did? He stole his neighbour's little lamb, and left him with nothing at all.

David That's outrageous! Just because he's rich, that doesn't mean he can do as he likes. I'll make him pay for it! I'll make him wish he'd never been born! Who is he?

Nathan It's you.

David Right! Call out the guard! I won't tolerate such . . .

Narrator Suddenly David stopped.

- He *blinked in astonishment*,
- he *scratched his head*,
- and then he *put his face in his hands*

David What did you say?

Nathan It's you. You've got a palace full of beautiful women. Uriah had just one wife, and because you're the king you thought you could take her.

Narrator David realised then what a terrible thing he had done, and he listened very quietly as Nathan went on talking.

Nathan You can't expect people to love you and respect you when you behave like this. I'm afraid you're in for a very bad time indeed.

David I deserve it. I'm really sorry.

Nathan And you'll be even sorrier.

Narrator And he was. But he changed, and eventually he became a great king.

God's Relief Airlift

Based on 1 Kings 17:1-6

BEFORE THE DAY

Obtain some names of prisoners of conscience – Amnesty International can provide a current list – and help the children write simple messages of support. Keep them simple, avoid contentious language, and let the children sign only their first names, e.g:

Dear X, I am sorry you are in prison, and am praying for you. Love from Tracey.

Send the letters off, but place copies of them on a board with perhaps some simple details of the recipient.

• Think about the actions for all the children to join in during the story.

ON THE DAY

Introduction

We're going to share some news of a very interesting project, soon. First, we'll say our 'Thank you Prayer'.

'Thank you' Prayer

Thank you, God, for all you give us,
thank you for the earth and sea,
thank you, God, for special people,
thank you, God, for making me.

God's Story

Hi there. Roddy's the name – Roddy Raven. Now, we get a bit of a bad press, we ravens. Just because we're black, and not all pretty colours like blue tits are, people have got this idea that we're bad. Let me tell you, though, we're very important, really; we could tell you such stories . . .

There was the time we were called in to help with famine relief. And the request came from the very top: higher than the Prime Minister – higher even than the Head of the Water Board. There! I knew you'd be impressed. Yes, this came right from Big G himself as we ravens call him – God to ordinary creatures like you. The creator of the universe needed a little bit of help, and who did he ask? Me. Caw! Not surprising, really. If you're looking for a combination of good flying skills, steady nerve and razor-sharp intelligence, you'll go a long way to find better than a raven.

The first I knew about it was when I was leading my squadron in a recce over some cornfields. To be honest, there wasn't much growing at the time and finding food was really hard – especially as the farmers were all the more determined to keep us away, greedy lot! We'd got the tactics worked out. Blue section swooped over the fields and distracted the farmer, and then the rest of us came in low behind him and had a feed. Then we swapped over. Anyway, it was just at that point that Control got in touch.

God told me there was a human prophet called Elijah who had got himself into trouble. You see he'd been speaking out of turn as far as the local king was concerned. That doesn't surprise me. King Ahab was a really bad lot. It wasn't much fun for anybody where he was in charge. So Elijah stood up to him and that's why he got into trouble.

'I've arranged for him to go and hide for a while,' God told me. 'Your mission is to keep him well fed.'

I knew the form straight away. A famine-relief airlift. God would provide the food, and our job was to get it delivered on target on time. So I got my chaps together. 'We're going to have to do some pretty nifty flying,' I told them. 'Human beings won't eat food if it's been dropped just anywhere. So you're going to have to practise precision drops. OK?'

Well, it wasn't a serious problem to my flyers. They'd been doing precision drops for years; just not with bread, that's all, but the principle's the same. So after a week's refresher training they were all ready to go. And not a moment too soon, either. Elijah had been shooting his mouth off again, telling the king that there was going to be a food shortage and it was all the king and queen's fault. Now anyone with any sense of diplomacy knows that you might think that kind of thing but you don't say it. Or not to a king like Ahab, anyway. So Elijah was legging it for all he was worth into the desert, and by the time we'd finished polishing up our precision flying he was sitting there with his tongue hanging out. There wasn't a moment to lose.

- So we *put on our goggles*,
- we *tested our wings*,
- and when everything was OK *(thumbs up)* we *took off*

Now it was important not to attract attention. When there's a food shortage, people notice things like large squadrons of ravens. So we went in in waves two minutes apart, flying low and fast to the target area. I don't mind telling you, my chaps are good, but the way Elijah could eat it was hard work keeping up with him. But then I often find that with the people who work for God; they really seem to enjoy his food (even if they don't always remember to say thank you). So wave after wave took off carrying as big a load as they could while the eagles provided a bit of high-altitude surveillance and protection. There was a nice clean patch of rock with an X marked on it and we had to land the food on that and then get away fast before either the next wave came in or Elijah gobbled it down and got impatient. Either way, things could turn ugly.

While most of us were doing this, I'd got a couple of spies at King Ahab's court, just eavesdropping to see whether there was likely to be trouble. The word I got back was that Ahab was hunting everywhere for Elijah – we'd have to be extra careful not to attract attention.

Obviously, all this could go on for a long time, and my flyers were showing signs of battle fatigue. Eventually, I knew I'd got to have a word with Control.

Just like God, of course, he knew exactly what the trouble was before I got there. 'Don't worry, Roddy, old chap,' he told me. 'You people have put on a jolly good show, and it's someone else's turn to help now.'

'Well, that's very good,' I said, 'but you aren't going to use just anybody are you? I mean, this is a very difficult and dangerous mission.'

'Absolutely,' God agreed. 'I've got just the person lined up – a widow in Zarephath who's nearly run out of food. She and Elijah can help each other.'

Well, I had my doubts, I don't mind admitting. This seemed too important a job to give to a human being with no feathers and a heavy bone structure. Still, that's the thing about God. Always full of surprises.

Our Story

Draw attention to the display.

To people imprisoned for their beliefs, a letter of support can be like bread from heaven. Terry Waite spoke movingly of a postcard he had received that gave him the will to live. Ask the other children if they would like to do something similar.

You could even start a Roddy Raven Club and make it a regular activity.

Prayers

We're Glad

Thank you, God,
for people who speak out
against unfairness and bullying.
Thank you for helping them,
and using them to make the world
better for all of us.

We're Sad

Please forgive us, God,
for pretending not to notice
when people need help.

Let's Pray for People

Please, God, bless and support
all the people who stand up
for others who are weaker.
Please show us how we can support them
both by our prayers
and our actions.

Songs

I come like a beggar
Make me a channel of your peace
Peace is flowing like a river
When I needed a neighbour

God's Relief Airlift

God's Story

Roddy   Hi there. Roddy Raven's the name. Now, ravens get a bit of a bad press, just because we're black, and not pretty colours like blue tits, but we're unsung heroes, we are. Take the time we were called in for famine relief. And it came from the very top: higher than the Prime Minister – higher even than the Head of the Water Board. There! I knew you'd be impressed. Yes, this came right from Big G himself as we ravens call him – God to ordinary creatures like you. Caw!

God   The point is, Roddy, I need a combination of good flying skills, steady nerve and razor-sharp intelligence.

Roddy   Then you'll go a long way to find better than a raven.

God   One of my prophets is in trouble with the king.

Roddy   That doesn't surprise me. King Ahab's a really bad lot.

God   I've arranged for Elijah to go and hide for a while. Your mission is to keep him well fed.

Roddy   I knew the form straight away. A famine-relief airlift. I got my chaps together for a top level briefing.

God   Human beings won't eat food if it's been dropped just anywhere. So go and practise precision drops. OK?

Roddy   Well, it wasn't a serious problem to my flyers. They'd been doing precision drops for years; just not with bread, that's all, but the principle's the same. So after a week's refresher training they were all ready to go.

God   And not a moment too soon, either. Elijah's just been blaming the king for the food shortage.

Roddy   Well, really! Anyone with any sense of diplomacy knows that you might think that kind of thing but you don't say it. Or not to a king like Ahab, anyway. There's obviously not a moment to lose.

- So we *put on our goggles,*
- we *tested our wings,*
- and when everything was OK *(thumbs up)* we *took off*

We went in in waves two minutes apart, flying low and fast to the target area. I don't mind telling you, my chaps are good, but the way Elijah could eat it was hard work keeping up with him.

God   My staff always enjoy my food, even if they don't always remember to say thank you.

Roddy   There was a nice clean patch of rock with an X marked on it and we had to land the food on that and then get away fast before either the next wave came in or Elijah gobbled it down and got impatient. Either way, things could turn ugly. My chaps are good, but even they began to show signs of battle fatigue.

God   Don't worry, Roddy, old chap. You've put on a jolly good show, and it's someone else's turn now. I've got just the person – a widow in Zarephath who's nearly run out of food. She and Elijah can help each other.

Roddy   What – a human being with no feathers and a heavy bone structure?

God   You know me, Roddy: always full of surprises.

A Piece of Cake

Based on 1 Kings 17:1-16

BEFORE THE DAY

Prepare a long list of household items, including such things as string, soap, sticking plasters, and some luxury items such as CDs and personal stereos. Make one copy for every six children in the class. Divide the class into groups of six, ensuring a good mix of children in each, and ask them to imagine they are going to live on a desert island, or perhaps get lost in a forest. They can choose, say, ten items to take with them. When they've listed their choices, stick them up on a board.

• Think about the actions for all the children to join in during the story.

ON THE DAY

Introduction

We're going to think this morning about how we decide what's important in life. First, we'll say our 'Thank you' prayer.

'Thank you' Prayer

Thank you, God, for all you give us,
thank you for the earth and sea;
thank you, God, for special people,
thank you, God, for making me.

God's Story

Elijah knew he was going to be in trouble, but then you have to get used to that when you're a prophet. He'd just told King Ahab that there was going to be nothing to eat for years. And not just for the king, either, but for everybody. Now it may seem strange, but people who bring bad news often get punished as if *they'd* made it happen. But this was worse. Elijah had said that the whole problem was King Ahab's fault – and if there's one thing that kings and governments hate even more than bad news,

it's being told that it's their fault. That, though, was precisely what Elijah had told the king.

'I think you'd better get away for a while,' God told Elijah. 'Give old Ahab a chance to cool off. I've got a place for you to hide with a nice stream there you can drink from, and I've arranged for your food to be flown in.'

Now, Elijah might have been a prophet, but even he couldn't see far enough ahead to know about aeroplanes. 'Flown in?' he asked.

'That's right,' God answered. 'I've got an arrangement with the local ravens: cheap, efficient and environmentally friendly. They'll keep you fed while you're there.'

They did, too – until the stream dried up. Even ravens can't go without water, so before long they had to move on and leave Elijah on his own. 'What am I going to do now?' thought Elijah.

'Come on,' said God. 'Pick your feet up and get going. There's a widow in the next town who's going to look after you.'

So Elijah did as God said.

Meanwhile, at the town of Zarephath, Martha was feeling very unhappy. She was a widow who lived with her little boy, Abe. She knew there was no food anywhere; all the shops had run out long ago, and nothing was growing in the fields. 'Well, Abe,' she said, 'it looks as though we'll be able to have one last meal. Let's try and make it a nice one, shall we?'

She went out to gather some wood for a fire, so that she could cook some special cakes with the flour she had left, and she saw a strange man in the street. He looked very dirty, as though nobody cared about him. 'He must have been living rough for a long time,' she thought. 'I wish I could help him, but what have I got to give him?' And she went on gathering sticks.

The man came over. 'Good morning,' he said. 'My name's Elijah. Can you spare me a little water?' She nodded and went off to fetch some from the well. 'Oh, and have you anything to eat?' he added.

Martha felt terrible. 'I really wish I could help,' she said, 'but I've just got enough for myself and my son to have one last meal before we die.'

'I'll tell you what,' Elijah answered. 'If you give me something to eat, I can promise you

God won't let you starve. There'll always be food in your jar, and oil to cook it with, until the crops grow again.'

Martha looked at him. 'I can't refuse him,' she thought. 'After all, what difference will a bit of cake make when we're starving anyway. And there again, he might be right; perhaps God will provide.'

'Go on in and sit down,' she said. 'I'll make a cake.' She gathered some wood and started a fire going. Then she took the last bit of flour, and the last few drops of oil that she had and made a nice little cake for the three of them to share.

'That was lovely,' Elijah said. 'You're a great cook.'

'I'm glad you liked it,' answered Martha. 'I wanted our last meal on earth to be special.'

Elijah just smiled knowingly and went outside to sleep under the stars. He'd grown to like that over the years: 'It's not exactly five-star,' he thought as he lay looking up at the night sky, 'but it's a terrific view.'

Next morning, Elijah woke up to the smell of Martha's cooking. 'I could get used to this,' he thought, 'if only God would let me.' He got up and followed his nose to where Martha was cooking some dough over a log fire. She smiled at him. 'I don't know what influence you've got,' she said, 'but you were right. We used the last of the flour and oil last night, and this morning there was more in the jars. What's the secret?'

'If I knew that,' said Elijah, 'I'd vacuum pack it – if I knew what vacuum packing meant.'

'Your God must be great to work for,' said Martha.

'Well, it's certainly not dull,' replied Elijah, wondering whether King Ahab was after him yet.

Elijah stayed at Zarephath for a long time, and although Martha made lots of cakes the jar of flour never ran out and there was always oil in the bottle. They all enjoyed Martha's cooking.

- Elijah would *chop wood for the fire*
- Martha would *mix the dough*
- Abe would *lick out the bowl*

They all became very good friends and life was happy even though they were never rich. One day, Martha said, 'I'm really glad I met you. I never thought I was going to be happy again.'

'Same here,' Elijah replied. 'Let's just say, God helped us to help each other.'

'No problem for God,' said Abe, 'a piece of cake!'

Our Story

Talk about the exercise you did in class, read out some of the lists and ask the wider group for comments. Notice how difficult it was to decide what was *really* important, and point out also how the children co-operated to help make the best choices. When people are poor they have to decide what's most important to them. And top of the list should be other people!

Prayers

We're Glad
Loving God,
it's so good to know
that all of us can help you
and help each other.
Thank you for giving us
families and friends.

We're Sad
We're sorry, God,
for when we've ignored people
who were in need;
or when we've said,
'I have so little to offer.'
Help us to trust you,
and share what little we have.

Let's Pray for People
Please God, help all people
who feel poor and helpless
to offer whatever they have
to each other and to you.
And help us to find ways
of getting involved in that.

Songs

A new commandment
Bind us together
Brother, sister, let me serve you
I come like a beggar
Love is like a circle
There are people who live in mansions
When God made the garden of creation

A Piece of Cake

God's Story

Narrator	Elijah knew he was going to be in trouble. He'd just told King Ahab that there was going to be nothing to eat for years, and it was all Ahab's fault. God was on Elijah's side, though.
God	I think you'd better get away for a while, Elijah. Give old Ahab a chance to cool off. I've got a place for you to hide with a nice stream you can drink from, and I've arranged for your food to be flown in.
Elijah	Flown in?
God	That's right. I've got an arrangement with the local ravens: cheap, efficient and environmentally friendly. They'll keep you fed while you're there.
Narrator	They did, too – until the stream dried up.
Elijah	What am I going to do now?
God	Come on, pick your feet up and get going. There's a widow in Zarephath who's going to look after you.
Narrator	That widow was feeling very unhappy. She lived with her little boy, Abe. She knew there was no food anywhere, and nothing was growing in the fields.
Martha	Well, Abe, let's have our last meal, shall we?
Narrator	She went out to gather some wood for a fire, so that she could cook some special cakes with the flour she had left, and she saw a strange man in the street. He looked very dirty, as though nobody cared about him.
Elijah	Hello, my name's Elijah. Can you spare a little water?
Martha	Of course. Wait here while I go to the well.

Elijah	Oh, and have you anything to eat?
Martha	I really wish I could help, but Abe and I've just got enough for one last meal before we die.
Elijah	I'll tell you what. If you give me something to eat, I can promise you God won't let you starve.
Martha	Oh well, what's a bit of cake when we're starving anyway?
Narrator	She used the last of the flour and oil that she had and made a nice little cake for the three of them to share. Then Elijah went outside to sleep under the stars.
Elijah	Maybe it's not exactly five-star, but it's a terrific view.
Narrator	When Elijah woke up, he could smell cooking.
Martha	I don't know what influence you've got, but the jars were full this morning. What's the secret?
Elijah	If I knew that, I'd vacuum pack it – if I knew what vacuum packing meant.
Narrator	Elijah stayed at Zarephath for a long time. The jar of flour never ran out and there was always oil in the bottle. They all enjoyed Martha's cooking.

- Elijah would *chop wood for the fire*
- Martha would *mix the dough*
- Abe would *lick out the bowl*

Martha	I never thought I was going to be happy again.
Elijah	Let's just say, God helped us to help each other.
Abe	It was a piece of cake.

God Loves Life

Based on 1 Kings 17:17-24

BEFORE THE DAY

What sorts of things make the children cross? Have they ever thought about telling God about them? Perhaps some of them would like to write their own prayers, not necessarily asking for answers but just letting off steam by telling God how they feel. Some of them could probably be used in the assembly.

• Think about the actions for all the children to join in during the story.

ON THE DAY

Introduction

We're going to think this morning about things that make us angry. First, though, we'll say our 'Thank you' Prayer.

'Thank you' Prayer

Thank you, God, for all you give us,
thank you for the earth and sea,
thank you, God, for special people,
thank you, God, for making me.

God's Story

I suppose you could say that Elijah was a refugee: running away from King Ahab who was after his blood (Ahab was always after *somebody's* blood) and staying with his friend Martha and her son, Abe. Of course, he could have been a lot less fortunate. Martha might have been one of those people who say to refugees, 'You keep away from my property.' But Martha wasn't like that; she helped Elijah and Elijah helped her, and they got on together really well.

When something went very badly wrong for her, though, even she blamed Elijah at first. This is what happened.

One day, Martha decided to do some spring cleaning. Elijah remembered an urgent meeting he had to go to, which he'd forgotten to mention before, and said that he was terribly sorry not to help but he wouldn't be home until late.

As Martha began her work, she noticed that Abe didn't seem quite himself. It was a lovely day, and normally he would have been out playing in the woods, but he was sitting in a corner of the house looking fed up.

'What's the matter?' asked Martha.

'Nothing,' Abe replied.

'Are you feeling ill?' Martha asked.

'I've got a headache, that's all. Leave me alone!' said Abe impatiently. Now Martha *knew* there was something wrong.

'You've got a bit of 'flu,' she told him. 'It always makes you bad-tempered.'

• Abe *shook his fist*
• and he *hunched his shoulders*
• and he *pulled an ugly face*!

'I'm not bad-tempered!' he shouted, going red in the face and stamping his foot for good measure.

'Oh, I'm sorry,' his mother replied. 'I can see now that I was mistaken.'

Abe went off to his room and sulked. Martha wasn't too worried; a good sleep would do him good, she thought. She had quite a good morning, turning out the cupboards and finding all sorts of treasures she had thought she'd lost, including three gold coins, two toothpicks and a box of Elijah's home-made corn plasters. Well, you do a lot of walking when you're a prophet.

When it came to lunch time, Abe was still in his room. Martha thought if he was sleeping it might be best not to disturb him. She could hear him snoring the way he always did when he had 'flu. So she put some food aside for him for when he woke up, and got on with washing the curtains.

It was about the middle of the afternoon when Martha realised that something was wrong. Everything seemed quiet. Too quiet. She put her head round Abe's door, and could just hear him breathing faintly. That could have been a sign he was getting better, but Martha didn't like it. It wasn't just quiet, it was shallow, as though the air was hardly getting into his body at all. She went over to him, and found that whereas he would usually have been feverish he was actually very cold.

Martha was frightened. She shook Abe to wake him up, but nothing happened. She shook him harder, and even started slapping his face with her hand – something she would never do usually – desperately trying to wake him. None of it worked. By now, Martha was in tears. She picked Abe up in her arms and carried him through to the living room where she sat on a chair and hugged him. She didn't know whether he could hear her or not, but just in case, she talked to him the whole time, telling him not to worry, and how much she loved him, begging him to open his eyes and tell her he was all right. But it didn't save Abe. Gradually, his breathing slowed right down and stopped. A few moments later, Elijah came breezing into the room all unawares: 'Hi, Martha! Had a good day?'

Martha snapped. 'I'll give you, "Hi, Martha"!' she burst out. 'I suppose this is what you prophets do, is it – go round looking for people God can punish? I know I'm not perfect but I don't deserve this.'

Elijah was horrified. He picked Abe up and carried him to his own room. He had a few things he wanted to say to God in private.

'Thanks a bunch, God!' he said, bitterly. 'This is how you thank Martha for being kind to me, is it? Fancy using a child to get to her!' Then he calmed down a bit, and tried to use his own breath to make Abe breathe. 'Please, God, let him live,' he said. 'Help him to breathe again.'

Now you might expect that God would be angry with Elijah for talking to him the way he did, but fortunately for a lot of us God's not like that. And as Elijah watched, he saw Abe's chest begin to move as he started breathing again.

When Elijah carried Abe back to Martha she nearly fainted with joy. She hugged and kissed Abe, and told him how much she loved him. Abe opened his eyes and looked at her.

'Oh, really, Mother! If you're going to start getting all soppy I'm going out into the woods. Coming, Elijah?'

Our Story

Ideally, the children's prayers should be used either as well as or instead of the ones below. They could also be put up on a display for other people to read. (Some of the writers might prefer to remain anonymous, and this should be respected.) Many children might feel it's not quite right to tell God we're angry, and it might be worth pointing out that we're only telling him what he already knows! He also knows how important it is for us to talk about our feelings. And he's a terrific listener!

Prayers

We're Glad

Thank you, God,
for loving and understanding.
Thank you for allowing us
to be completely honest with you.

We're Sad

Sometimes, God, we don't tell you
how we're really feeling.
We're afraid to, because we think
you might not like it.
But you know anyway!
Forgive us for not trusting you,
and help us to be really honest with you.

Let's Pray for People

We pray for people who are really angry,
but have no one to shout at;
for those who want to blame someone,
and end up blaming themselves.
Please, God, help all people to trust you,
and to unload their feelings onto you
without fear.

Songs

God sends a rainbow
God's love is deeper
He's got the whole world in his hands
Jesus had all kinds of friends
Jesus' love is very wonderful

God Loves Life

God's Story

Narrator	Elijah the prophet was a refugee from the wicked king Ahab, and he was being sheltered by his friend Martha and her son Abe. One day, Martha decided to do some spring cleaning. Elijah remembered an urgent meeting he had to go to, which he'd forgotten to mention before, and said that he was terribly sorry not to help but he wouldn't be home until late. As Martha began her work, she noticed that Abe didn't seem quite himself.
Martha	What's the matter?
Abe	Nothing.
Martha	Are you feeling ill?
Abe	*(Impatiently)* I've got a headache, that's all. Leave me alone!
Martha	You've got 'flu. It always makes you bad-tempered.
Narrator	Abe *shook his fist* and he *hunched his shoulders* and he *pulled an ugly face*!
Abe	*(Shouting, and stamping his foot)* I'm not bad-tempered!
Martha	Oh, I'm sorry. I can see now that I was mistaken.
Narrator	Abe went off to his room and sulked. When it came to lunch time, he was still there. Martha thought if he was sleeping it might be best not to disturb him. She could hear him snoring the way he always did when he had 'flu. So she put some food aside for him for when he woke up, and got on with washing the curtains. It was about the middle of the afternoon when Martha realised that something was wrong.
Martha	This is awful. He's hardly breathing!

Narrator	Martha was frightened. She shook Abe to wake him up, but nothing happened. Martha was in tears. She picked Abe up in her arms and carried him through to the living room where she sat on a chair and hugged him. Gradually, Abe's breathing slowed right down and stopped. A few moments later, Elijah came breezing into the room all unawares:
Elijah	Hi, Martha! Had a good day?
Martha	I'll give you, 'Hi, Martha'! I suppose this is what you prophets do, is it – go round looking for people God can punish? I know I'm not perfect but I don't deserve this.
Narrator	Elijah was horrified. He picked Abe up and carried him to his own room. He had a few things he wanted to say to God in private.
Elijah	Thanks a bunch, God! This is how you thank Martha for being kind to me, is it? Fancy using a child to get to her!
Narrator	Now you might expect that God would be angry with Elijah for talking to him the way he did, but fortunately for a lot of us God's not like that. And as Elijah watched, Abe started breathing again. Martha nearly fainted with joy. She hugged and kissed Abe, and told him how much she loved him.
Abe	Oh, really, Mother! If you're going to start getting all soppy I'm going out to play. Coming, Elijah?

'They're Out to Get Me'

1 Kings 19:1-18

BEFORE THE DAY

We often think of God as big, powerful and frightening. Can the children think of gentle images for God: a smile, a helping hand, the light of a candle, etc? Can they draw them, to make a visual display for the assembly?

• Think about the actions for all the children to join in during the story.

ON THE DAY

Introduction

We're going to think about what God is like in a few moments. First, we'll say our 'Thank you' Prayer.

'Thank you' Prayer

Thank you, God, for all you give us,
thank you for the earth and sea;
thank you, God, for special people,
thank you, God, for making me.

God's Story

Although King Ahab and Queen Jezebel had committed some simply dreadful crimes, they still thought that the prophet Elijah should be nice to them, but he just kept telling them off for the wrong things they had done. 'Don't mix religion and politics,' they used to say. They really believed they could do as they liked and God didn't mind – just because they were the nation's leaders! Silly people! Anyway, one day Queen Jezebel sent a note to Elijah saying, 'I'm fed up with you criticising me. I've told you to stop and you haven't. So now I'm going to get you for it.'

Well, Elijah didn't hang around to find out whether she meant it. He packed up his bags, picked up his feet and ran like a hare with a fox on its tail until he came to a cave in the mountains. 'Here's a good place to hide,' he thought.

Just as Elijah was getting the cave ship-shape for the night, he heard God speaking to him. 'Elijah,' said God, 'what are you doing here?'

'I'm hiding,' said Elijah. 'Everyone has turned against you. They've torn down all the churches, killed all the holy people. I'm the only one left who still loves you. And now they're after me!'

'Oh dear!' thought God. 'Another silly man who thinks he's the only one who's right.' Then he spoke to Elijah again.

'Elijah, I want you to go and stand at the front of the cave.'

Elijah wondered what was going on, but he wasn't up to arguing with God. So out he went, but as he got outside he was nearly blown off his feet. An enormous wind sprang up and went whistling through the valley. Elijah nearly got blown off the ledge he was standing on. He huddled against the rock and wanted to go back inside the cave, but he knew he had to stay there as God had told him.

• So he *pulled his cloak around him*
• he *hunched his shoulders*
• and he *closed his eyes, tightly*

'I expect God is going to speak to me in this great strong wind,' he thought. But God was not in the wind.

Soon, the wind stopped and Elijah thought, 'Thank goodness that's over!' Just as he was thinking it, the earth began to shake – just a little at first, but it soon got stronger. And before long everything was rocking and shaking and great big cracks were appearing in the rocks around Elijah. 'Wow!' he thought, as he crouched in a terrified huddle against the mountain, 'God must have something really important to say.' But God wasn't in the earthquake, either.

After the earthquake, Elijah was just getting his breath back when there was a sudden flash and the whole world seemed to be on fire. Elijah couldn't understand how he survived it: everything seemed to be burning furiously, the trees, the grass – even the sky itself seemed to be a raging inferno. But still God didn't seem to be around. Elijah was very puzzled.

The fire died down and everything went quiet. Elijah waited for whatever was coming next – perhaps a great flood, or a blizzard, or maybe a stampede of wild animals – but there was nothing. Absolute silence. Elijah decided to go back into the cave. Perhaps in the morning he would realise it had all been a dream. Gosh, but it was quiet! It was one of those silences when you get the feeling that something is going to happen, but Elijah was just too tired to bother. So he went back into his cave, and then he heard it. A soft, gentle whisper. A tiny little voice. 'Who's that?' he thought. 'Not one of the queen's men, I hope.' He stood very still and listened, and he heard it again. Then he realised it was God. Well, fancy that! All that ear-splitting noise and terrifying power, where any sensible person would have expected God to be speaking, and all the time Elijah was supposed to be listening for a tiny little voice!

Elijah was rather scared by all this, and he wrapped his cloak around his head and went back to the cave entrance, peering through the folds of his cloak like a frightened child! Then God spoke again. 'What are you doing here, Elijah? Why aren't you at home?'

'I can't stay there!' said Elijah. 'They've killed all the prophets, broken all your rules – I'm the only one left who cares about you – and now they're out to get me, as well.'

'Don't flatter yourself!' said God, 'You're not the only one who's got it right, by a long way.'

'Well it feels that way,' said Elijah, sulkily.

'Go back,' said God. 'You'll find I've got quite a lot of friends out there. Some of them are going to take over as great leaders, and the evil people won't have the power any more. So you've nothing to be afraid of. "Only one" indeed! There are a good seven thousand more like you – so stop feeling sorry for yourself and go back to join them.'

So Elijah went back. Things didn't change instantly, and Elijah still upset the king and queen by what they called 'interfering in politics', but God was always Elijah's friend and Elijah learnt to trust him. He didn't see fires and earthquakes every day – but he often heard that tiny, whispering voice.

Our Story

Draw attention to the display and ask the children for other signs of a gentle, whispering God, in creation.

Prayers

We're Glad

Thank you, God,
for not shouting all the time.
Thank you for being gentle,
and for speaking to us
in a tiny, whispering voice.

We're Sad

We do get a bit power mad at times, God.
It's easy to get carried away,
to be easily impressed by people
who are strong, or loud.
Forgive us for forgetting
that quietness is important, too.

Let's Pray for People

Please, God,
bless the people who are frightened of you:
people who think you're merely powerful,
like thunder and lightning.
Help them to know that you're gentle, too,
like the whisper of the breeze,
and that no one needs to be afraid of you.

Songs

Be still and know
Be still, for the presence of the Lord
'Cheep!' said the sparrow
Morning has broken
This little light of mine

'They're Out to Get Me'

God's Story

Narrator Although King Ahab and Queen Jezebel were really bad people, they still thought that the prophet Elijah should be nice to them, but he just kept telling them off. Finally, he had to run away to a cave in the mountains. Just after he arrived, he heard God speaking to him.

God Elijah, what are you doing here?

Elijah I'm hiding. Everyone's against you. They've destroyed all the churches, killed all the prophets. I'm the only one friend you have left. And now they're after me!

God *(Aside)* Oh dear! Another silly man who thinks he's the only one who's right. *(To Elijah)* Elijah, I want you to go and stand at the front of the cave.

Narrator Elijah went outside and was nearly blown off his feet by a strong wind blowing up and down the valley. He huddled against the rock and wanted to go back inside the cave, but he knew he had to stay there as God had told him.

- So he *pulled his cloak around him*
- he *hunched his shoulders*
- and he *closed his eyes, tightly*

Elijah I expect God will speak in this great strong wind.

Narrator But God was not in the wind.

Elijah Thank goodness that's over! Oh, no! an earthquake!

Narrator Before long everything was rocking and shaking around Elijah as he huddled against the mountainside.

But God wasn't in the earthquake, either. Elijah was just getting his breath back when there was a sudden flash and the whole world seemed to be on fire. But still

God didn't seem to be around. Elijah was very puzzled. The fire died down and everything went quiet. Then he heard it. A soft, gentle whisper.

Elijah Who's that? Well, fancy that! All that ear-splitting noise and terrifying power, where any sensible person would have expected God to be speaking, and all the time I was supposed to be listening for a tiny little voice!

Narrator Elijah was rather scared by all this, and he wrapped his cloak around his head and went back to the cave entrance, peering through the folds of his cloak like a frightened child!

God Why are you here, Elijah? Why aren't you at home?

Elijah I can't stay there! They've killed all the prophets, broken all your rules – I'm the only one left who cares about you – and now they're out to get me, as well.

God Don't flatter yourself! You're not the only one who's got it right, by a long way. Go back. You'll find I've got quite a lot of friends out there. Some of them are going to take over as great leaders, and the evil people won't have the power any more. So you've nothing to be afraid of. 'Only one' indeed! There are a good seven thousand more like you – so stop feeling sorry for yourself and go back to join them.

Narrator So Elijah went back. Things didn't change instantly, and Elijah still upset the king and queen by what they called 'interfering in politics', but God was always Elijah's friend and Elijah learnt to trust him. He didn't see fires and earthquakes every day – but he often heard that tiny, whispering voice.

Shaphat!

Based on 1 Kings 19:15-21

BEFORE THE DAY

Ask the children about their 'heroes': sports or media personalities, or whatever. Notice how many of these will be members of teams or groups. Where they are not, ask the children what other people those heroes need: producers, camera crews, trainers, managers, etc. None of us is ever truly self-sufficient. Prepare a picture display, with captions, for the assembly.

• Think about the actions for all the children to join in during the story.

ON THE DAY

Introduction

We're going to hear a story soon about someone who thought he was all alone, and then found out that he wasn't. First, we'll say our 'Thank you' prayer.

'Thank you' Prayer

Thank you, God, for all you give us,
thank you for the earth and sea;
thank you, God, for special people,
thank you, God, for making me.

God's Story

'It's all right for you, God,' Elijah complained. 'You're immortal – and if King Ahab and Queen Jezebel have their way, you and I are both going to find out what a difference that makes.'

'Oh, stop worrying about Ahab and Jezebel,' said God. 'Why do you prophetic types always get so carried away? I suppose you think you're the only friend I've got in the world!'

'I *know* I am!' replied Elijah. 'Take a look around and you'll see. The people have broken all their promises to you, torn down your places of worship, killed all your prophets, and I'm the only one left.'

'Don't flatter yourself,' God answered, 'and stop feeling sorry for yourself at the same time. "Only one left", indeed! I want you to go back to Damascus by the desert road.'

'I'd rather go to Morocco,' said Elijah, 'then I'd be Morocco bound.'

'Less of that,' said God. 'I've earmarked that line for a Hope and Crosby musical, and I didn't give you prophetic powers so you could pinch their jokes.'

'Sorry, God,' said Elijah. 'I'll just go to Damascus.'

'And when you get there,' said God, 'be careful what you say. I don't want you upsetting the future kings.'

'Future kings?'

'Yes, you're to anoint Hazael as king of Aram and Jehu as king of Israel.'

'Jehu?' asked Elijah. 'Isn't he the one with the sports chariot: lowered suspension, wide wheels and custom paint job?'

'That's the one,' said God. 'Drives like a madman, so don't go accepting any lifts. And while you're there, you're to anoint Elisha to be your successor as prophet. Between them, they'll take care of the trouble-makers. Any that get away from Hazael will be dealt with by Jehu.'

'Sort of, wicket keeper and long stop?' Elijah interrupted.

'I've told you before about misusing your prophetic powers,' God scolded him. 'Any that still get away will be stopped by Elisha. And if you say anything about silly mid-off . . .'

When Elijah eventually got to Elisha's house, he knocked on the door and it was answered by a man of about his age. 'This is a bit silly,' he thought. 'I'd have expected God to choose a young man to take over from me.'

'Hello,' he said, 'I'm Elijah.'

'Shaphat!' said the other man.

'Bless you!' said Elijah. 'Is your name Elisha?'

'Shaphat!' repeated the other.

'My, my, what a terrible cold. I hope you get better soon. Now, it's like this, Elisha –'

'Shaphat!' the man roared.

'This is ridiculous!' thought Elijah. 'This man's in no fit state to be a prophet. A cough it, perhaps, but not a prophet. I'll try just once more.'

He put on his best smile: 'It's like this, Elisha –'

'Shaphat!' the man bellowed. 'You deaf or something? I keep telling you my name's Shaphat. You want my son. He's out in the fields over there. You'll know which one's him – he's always last.'

'Well, I do think God might have warned me,' thought Elijah. 'It's an easy enough mistake to make.' But he didn't say any more as he hurried off to the field. There he saw twelve ploughs being pulled by pairs of oxen. He went to the man guiding the last pair, and said, 'You must be Elisha.'

'Shaphat!' the man roared. 'I beg your pardon – terrible cold.'

It was, wasn't it! Would you like to do a big sneeze?

Divide up the group into three. On the command, one group will shout 'Russia!' another 'Tissue!' and a third group can shout 'Shaphat!' it should be quite something!

When the man had recovered, he said, 'Yes, I'm Elisha; what can I do for you?'

Elijah took off his special prophet's cloak and placed it on Elisha's shoulders. Elisha immediately understood what it meant. 'Look,' he said, 'I don't mind giving prophecy a go, but I'd really like to go and say good-bye to my father and mother first.'

'Who's stopping you?' grunted Elijah, 'just as long as you're coming into this business with your eyes open.'

So Elisha went back and hugged and kissed his parents good-bye, and then came back to where Elijah was waiting.

'Just one more job to do first,' he said. 'How about a barbecue?'

'Sounds okay to me,' Elijah replied.

'Good,' said Elisha, and he called all his friends who were ploughing with him. 'Come and get stuck in,' he called. 'Perhaps a good square meal will do us all some good.

SHAPHAT!'

'Bless you!' said Elijah.

Our Story

Point out the display, and the different ways people co-operate together (including the ones who made the display, of course). Ask the children what other people *they* need in their lives.

Prayers

We're Glad

Thank you, God,
for giving us each other.
Thank you for making us the kind of people
who work better together than apart.

We're Sad

Sometimes, God, we try to go it alone.
We think we don't need anybody else.
Please forgive us if we shut people
out of our lives,
and help us to appreciate each other.

Let's Pray for People

Loving God,
bless all people with difficult jobs to do;
all who feel lonely and neglected,
as though they were coping all alone.
Help us to be willing friends and helpers
to people who need encouragement.

Songs

A new commandment
Bind us together, Lord
Jesus had all kinds of friends
Jesus put this song into our hearts
When I needed a neighbour

Shaphat!

God's Story

Narrator   The prophet Elijah wasn't happy.

Elijah   It's all right for you, God, you're immortal – and if King Ahab and Queen Jezebel have their way . . .

God   Oh, stop worrying about Ahab and Jezebel. I suppose you think you're the only friend I've got in the world!

Elijah   I know I am! Take a look around and you'll see.

God   Don't flatter yourself. 'Only one left', indeed! I want you to go back to Damascus by the desert road.

Elijah   I'd rather go to Morocco, then I'd be 'Morocco bound'.

God   Hey! I've earmarked that line for a Hope and Crosby musical, and I didn't give you prophetic powers to pinch their jokes.

Elijah   Sorry, God. I'll just go to Damascus.

God   And when you get there, you're to anoint Hazael as king of Aram and Jehu as king of Israel.

Elijah   Jehu? Isn't he the one with the sports chariot: lowered suspension, wide wheels and custom paint job?

God   That's the one. Drives like a madman, so don't go accepting any lifts. And while you're there, you're to anoint Elisha as the next prophet.

Narrator   When Elijah eventually got to Elisha's house, he knocked on the door and a man answered.

Elijah   Hello, I'm Elijah.

Shaphat   Shaphat.

Elijah	Bless you! Is your name Elisha?
Shaphat	Shaphat!
Elijah	My, what a terrible cold. Now, it's like this, Elisha –
Shaphat	*(Shouts)* Shaphat! You deaf or something? I keep telling you my name's Shaphat. My son's out in the fields.
Narrator	Elijah hurried off to the field.
Elijah	You must be Elisha.
Elisha	Shaphat! I beg your pardon – terrible cold.
Narrator	It was, wasn't it! Would you like to do a big sneeze?
	Divide up the group into three. On the command, one group will shout 'Russia!' another 'Tissue!' and a third group can shout 'Shaphat!'
Elisha	Yes, I'm Elisha; what can I do for you?
Narrator	Elijah took off his special prophet's cloak and placed it on Elisha's shoulders. Elisha immediately understood.
Elisha	Look, I don't mind giving prophecy a go, but I'd like to go and say good-bye to my father and mother first.
Elijah	Who's stopping you? Just as long as you're coming into this business with your eyes open.
Narrator	So Elisha went back and hugged and kissed his parents good-bye, and then came back to Elijah.
Elisha	Before we go, how about a barbecue with my friends? A good square meal may do us all good. SHAPHAT!
Elijah	Bless you!

Corruption in High Places

Based on 1 Kings 21:1-25

BEFORE THE DAY

Tell the group the essence of the story, and work with them on a letter of protest to King Ahab. Stress the importance of being polite, even to people like that; keep the letter short and to the point; write it in a big hand on a large sheet of paper and invite the children to sign it. Before the assembly, put it up on prominent display.

• Think about the actions for all the children to join in during the story.

ON THE DAY

Introduction

We're going to hear a story about a very cruel and wicked king. But first, we'll say our 'Thank you' Prayer.

'Thank you' Prayer

Thank you, God, for all you give us,
thank you for the earth and sea;
thank you, God, for special people,
thank you, God, for making me.

God's Story

King Ahab lived in a wonderful palace with a lovely big garden. He was married to the beautiful Queen Jezebel, who was a grade one, fully paid-up member of the Let's be Horrible to Everyone Club. One day, she noticed that their neighbour Naboth had some very nice vines with big juicy grapes. Jezebel thought, 'Why should an unimportant person like him have that beautiful vineyard? It's good enough for a king and queen, that is.' When they were having dinner that evening, she said to Ahab, 'Just imagine – if you had that land you could grow your own vegetables.'

'The trouble is, though,' Ahab replied, 'that land belongs to Naboth's family and it's against the law for him to sell it.'

'Law? Law?' shrieked Jezebel. 'You're the king, aren't you! Are you going to allow some silly law someone else made to stop you getting what you want? You're pathetic!'

'You're absolutely right,' said Ahab. 'What's the point of being king if I can't have whatever I want?' So next morning Ahab went to see Naboth in his vineyard. 'I've decided that I'm going to have this land,' he said.

'Come again?' said Naboth.

'This land,' said Ahab. 'I want it.'

'Well, tha can't 'ave it!' said Naboth flatly, and carried on hoeing.

Ahab thought he must have been hearing things. 'I don't think I understand,' he said.

• Naboth *leaned on his hoe*
• Then he *scratched his head*
• Then he *wagged his finger* in Ahab's face

'Oh, is that reet?' he said. 'Well, let me mek it clear for thee. This land was me grandfather's afore me father 'ad it, and now it's mine. Tha can't 'ave it! And I'll tell thee summat else: there's bin a lot o' snails round 'ere, so tell that woman o' yourn to quit chuckin' 'em ower t'fence.'

Ahab didn't know what to say. He knew that Naboth was right about the land – and about the snails, if the truth be told. So he went inside, lay on his bed and sulked.

'What's the matter with you?' asked Jezebel.

'Naboth won't sell me his land,' whined Ahab.

'Oh, won't he now!' rejoined Jezebel. 'We'll see about that.' And she went downstairs to write some letters. Using Ahab's own personal notepaper, she wrote to the local magistrates and governors, telling them she wanted Naboth put on trial for a crime. 'Bribe a few of those lower-class common people,' she said, 'to say that Naboth is guilty of blasphemy – then you can have him stoned to death.'

Of course, Naboth tried to defend himself.

'What, me?' he protested. 'I never did nowt o' t'sort. It's that Jezebel what's be'ind this – well she'll not get me vineyard this road.'

But she did.

Next morning, Jezebel said to Ahab, 'You can go and walk in *your* vineyard, now. That ridiculous little Naboth fellow is dead.'

Ahab was thrilled to bits. After all, he thought, compared with the king, Naboth wasn't important.

But he was.

Elijah the prophet was just settling down to a date cookie and a glass of pineapple juice when he heard a voice.

'Elijah,' said the voice, 'do try to eat and drink more quietly when I'm talking to you.'

'Sorry, God,' said Elijah. 'I didn't know you were there.'

'Oh, don't be tiresome!' said God. 'How many times must I tell you, I'm *always* here – I just don't talk as much as some people I could mention, that's all.'

'I'm listening,' said Elijah, through a mouthful of dates.

'Well, I hope your ears are less blocked up than your mouth is,' God answered. 'I want you to listen very carefully. It's about the king.'

'Oh, no! Not the king!' moaned Elijah. 'What's he been up to now? Whatever it was, I bet that painted lady he married has something to do with it.'

'Yes, she has,' God said. 'But don't let him pass the buck – he knows what he's doing. He's stolen Naboth's vineyard.'

'I had an idea that might happen,' said Elijah. 'I'll go and tell him to give it back.'

'Why don't you let your ears do the work for a change, then your mouth can concentrate on eating?' said God. 'They killed Naboth to get the vineyard.'

'They what! You wait until I get my hands on them!' shouted Elijah.

'Really, Elijah!' said God. 'That's a waste of perfectly good cookie crumbs – you know the birds round here only eat wholemeal. Look, you can leave the judging and sentencing to me – all I want you to do is go and tell those two they're not going to get away with it.'

Elijah swallowed his cookie as fast as he could, drank his pineapple juice and set off for the palace. I won't tell you the details of what he said to Ahab and Jezebel, but by the time he'd finished with them they hated him even more than they had before!

Our Story

Show the group the protest letter, again pointing out how polite it is – insulting people isn't normally a good way of persuading them! Invite any other children who feel angry about what happened to Naboth to come and sign their names on the letter. When they're older, they will find situations when similar letters might be in order to present-day people.

Prayers

We're Glad

Thank you, God,
for using people like Elijah
to stand up for what is right.

We're Sad

We're sorry, God,
for any time that we've tried to get our way
by shouting more loudly
or taking advantage of others.
Help us to remember
that you care for everybody,
and that being fair to others
will make us happier, too.

Let's Pray for People

Please God, bless all people,
rich and poor,
strong and weak,
and help those of us who have a little more
to share with those who have a lot less.

Songs

Make me a channel of your peace
There are people who live in mansions
There's a great big world out there
When God made the garden of creation

Corruption in High Places

God's Story

Narrator	King Ahab lived in a wonderful palace with a lovely big garden. He was married to the beautiful but horrible Queen Jezebel. One day, she noticed that their neighbour Naboth had a very nice garden.
Jezebel	Ahab, wouldn't you like to have that garden?
Ahab	It belongs to Naboth, and I know he won't sell it.
Jezebel	Won't sell it? You're the king, aren't you? Make him!
Narrator	So Ahab went to see Naboth in his garden.
Ahab	I've come to tell you that I want this land.
Naboth	Well, tha can't 'ave it!
Ahab	I don't think I understand.
Narrator	• Naboth *leaned on his hoe* • Then he *scratched his head* • Then he *wagged his finger* in Ahab's face
Naboth	I said, tha can't 'ave it! And I'll tell thee summat else: there's bin a lot o' snails round 'ere, so tell that woman o' yourn to quit chuckin' 'em ower t'fence.
Narrator	Ahab went inside and moaned at Jezebel.
Ahab	*(Whines)* Naboth won't sell me his land.
Jezebel	Oh, won't he now! We'll see about that.
Narrator	Jezebel arranged for Naboth to be accused of a crime, so that he could be put to death. Of course, Naboth tried to defend himself.
Naboth	I never did nowt o' t'sort. It's that Jezebel what's be'ind this – well she'll not get me garden this road.

Narrator   But she did.

Jezebel   Ahab, darling, you can go and walk in *your* garden, now. That ridiculous little Naboth fellow is dead.

Narrator   Elsewhere, Elijah the prophet was just settling down to a date cookie when he heard a voice.

God   Elijah, please eat more quietly when I'm talking to you.

Elijah   Sorry, God, I didn't know you were there.

God   Oh, don't be tiresome! I'm *always* here.

Elijah   I'm listening.

God   Well, I hope your ears are less blocked up than your mouth is. It's about Ahab. He's stolen Naboth's garden.

Elijah   I'll go and tell him to give it back.

God   Too late. They killed Naboth to get the garden.

Elijah   They what! You wait until I get my hands on them!

God   Really, Elijah! That's a waste of perfectly good cookie crumbs – you know the birds round here only eat wholemeal. Look, you can leave the judging and sentencing to me – all I want you to do is go and tell those two they're not going to get away with it.

Narrator   Elijah swallowed his cookie as fast as he could, drank his pineapple juice and set off for the palace. I won't tell you the details of what he said to Ahab and Jezebel, but by the time he'd finished with them, they hated him even more than they had before!

Elisha's Oil Well

Based on 2 Kings 4:1-7

BEFORE THE DAY

Get the children to think about the people they might turn to for help. Let them draw pictures of police, 'lollipop' men and women, doctors, shopkeepers, clergy – anyone identifiable, who might help them if they needed it. Put the pictures up before the assembly.

• Think about the actions for all the children to join in during the story.

ON THE DAY

Introduction

We're going to hear a story in a few minutes about how a community came together to solve a problem. First, we'll say our 'Thank you' Prayer.

'Thank you' Prayer

Thank you, God, for all you give us,
thank you for the earth and sea;
thank you, God, for special people,
thank you, God, for making me.

God's Story

'I've got her now,' thought Joe. 'That Abbi woman's going to have to do whatever I want from now on.'

Joe was a loan-shark, and as if he didn't make enough money from that he did a bit of slave-trading on the side. One of his loan clients was Abbi, the widow of a prophet who had recently been killed. Lots of people had been going round to say how sorry they were, and to offer whatever help they could. So when Abbi heard another knock on the door, she was very pleased to open it.

'Joe!' she smiled. 'How nice of you to call.'

'Never mind that,' snarled Joe. 'What about my money?'

'Surely you can wait a few days?' Abbi gasped. 'I'll pay you as soon as we've sorted out my husband's affairs.'

'Oh, don't you come the poor widow act with me,' Joe sneered. 'I know you've got something put by.'

'Honestly, I haven't,' Abbi assured him, 'but as soon as I can I'll find a way to pay you.'

'Not good enough,' said Joe, flatly. 'Either you pay me the money, or I find another way of getting it back. How are those sons of yours?'

Abbi's blood ran cold. 'You wouldn't take them?'

'Nice, fit young men they are – fetch a nice price at the slave market, they would. You have the money by the weekend or I'm taking them.'

What was Abbi to do? She knew she couldn't possibly pay Joe back so quickly.

Joe knew it, too. In fact, he was banking on it. Abbi's sons would fetch a lot more at the market than she owed him, and then he'd be able to keep on threatening her and make her do anything he wanted. He couldn't wait for the weekend to come, when he was sure she wouldn't have the money.

Abbi only knew one person who might be able to help her. So she put on her hat and scarf and went out to find Elisha, the chief prophet. She knew he would want to help.

'That dreadful leech!' exclaimed Elisha when he heard the story. 'Whatever it takes, I'll keep his hands off your family!'

'I knew you'd help,' said Abbi with relief. 'I'll pay you back as soon as I can.'

• She *dried her eyes*
• she *put on her best smile*
• and she *held out her hand* for the money

Elisha shook his head. 'I'm not going to lend you the money,' he said. 'That way, you'd still be in debt. No, we've got to sort this out once and for all. What have you got in your house?'

'Nothing of any value,' Abbi wept. 'All I've got is a jar of oil for cooking, and somehow the three of us have to live on that!'

Elisha's eyes lit up. Oil! 'Go home,' he said to her, 'and borrow all the pots and jugs you can, and pour the oil out of the jar into them.'

'I've got a *jar* of oil,' Abbi said. 'Not a well of it.'

'Just trust God,' Elisha replied.

Abbi went back and called her two sons. 'Josh, you go down this side of the street and borrow anything that'll hold liquid,' she said. 'Nick, you go the other way and do the same.' Nick returned first with two large vases. Even one of them on its own was much bigger than the jar of oil, and Abbi wondered what on earth Elisha was playing at. Still, she did as he said and began to pour the oil out of the jar into the first of the vases. How strange: the oil just kept on coming! Soon, the vase was completely full and she had to start on the second one. But the oil jar was still full, as well.

Just then, Josh came in. 'I've got these cooking pots,' he said, 'but old Eva down the road says you be sure to return hers.'

'Of course I will!' replied Abbi, and started to pour. Still the oil jar was full, and the oil just went pouring out into the two pots. Josh and Nick got very fit that day; they couldn't borrow the containers fast enough. And all the time, Abbi just stood there pouring oil from the tiny jar and filling the enormous vessels. Eventually, they had to stop. The neighbours had run out of pots! Then Abbi made a big sign to put outside the house: 'Oil for heating and cooking. Best prices in town.' The word spread that Abbi's oil was cheaper and better than anyone else's, and she even had to send for Elisha to help serve the customers!

Come the weekend, Joe was knocking on the door with handcuffs and leg-irons at the ready.

'Bring out your sons!' he shouted, with a mean grin on his face.

Abbi went to the door. 'Never mind my boys,' she said. 'Here's your money, with interest. Now get out, and don't go peddling your loans around here any more. From now on, my neighbours and I are helping each other. We don't need your sort.'

Joe was very unhappy. What was he going to do? If he lost his business, he might even end up having to go to a loan shark himself!

Our Story

Ask the assembly to look at the pictures. Can they add any more ideas? They've probably been so busy trying to think of 'official' people, they've not thought of themselves or each other. But it was the whole community that sorted Joe out, wasn't it?

Prayers

We're Glad

Thank you, God,
for people who trust you
and help one another.

We're Sad

Sometimes we could do more than we do
to help people in trouble.
Please forgive us, God,
and show us the best way
to be helpful.

Let's Pray for People

Some people are so poor
that others can easily take advantage.
Please God, help all people
to be good neighbours
and help each other out of love,
not out of greed.

Songs

A new commandment
Brother, sister, let me serve you
Give me joy in my heart
I'm black, I'm white, I'm short, I'm tall
When I needed a neighbour

Elisha's Oil Well

God's Story

Narrator Joe was a loan-shark, and as if he didn't make enough money from that he did a bit of slave-trading on the side. One of his loan clients was Abbi, the widow of a prophet who had recently been killed. Lots of people had been going round to say how sorry they were, and to offer whatever help they could. So when Abbi heard another knock on the door, she was very pleased to open it.

Abbi Joe! How nice of you to call.

Joe Never mind that. What about my money?

Abbi Surely you can wait a few days? I'll pay you as soon as we've sorted out my husband's affairs.

Joe Oh, don't you come the poor widow act with me. I know you've got something put by.

Abbi Honestly, I haven't, but as soon as I can I'll find a way to pay you.

Joe Not good enough. Either you pay me the money, or I'll sell your sons at the slave market.

Narrator Abbi knew she couldn't possibly pay Joe back so quickly. Joe was banking on it: her sons would fetch a lot more at the market than she owed him. He couldn't wait for the weekend to come, when he was sure she wouldn't have the money. Desperately, Abbi told her story to Elisha, the chief prophet.

Elisha That dreadful leech! Whatever it takes, I'll keep Joe's hands off your family!

Narrator Abbi was thrilled.

- She *dried her eyes*
- she *put on her best smile*
- and she *held out her hand* for the money

Elisha	I'm not going to lend you the money. We've got to sort this out once and for all. What have you got at home?
Abbi	Nothing I can sell – just a jar of oil for cooking, and somehow the three of us have to live on that!
Elisha	Oil! Go home, and borrow all the pots and jugs you can, and pour the oil out of the jar into them.
Abbi	I've got a *jar* of oil, not a well of it.
Elisha	Just trust God.
Abbi	My sons can help. Josh, you go down this side of the street and borrow anything that'll hold liquid. Nick, you go the other way and do the same.
Narrator	Soon, Abbi had dozens of pots. And no matter how many she filled, the oil jar was still full. It was a miracle! Abbi made a big sign to put outside the house: 'Oil for heating and cooking. Best prices in town'. Come the weekend, Joe was knocking on the door with handcuffs and leg-irons at the ready.
Joe	Bring out your sons!
Abbi	Never mind my boys. Here's your money, with interest. Now get out of here, and don't go peddling your loans around here any more. From now on, my neighbours and I are helping each other. We don't need your sort.
Narrator	Joe was very unhappy. What was he going to do? If he lost his business, he might even end up having to go to a loan shark himself!

Walking Through Fire for God

Based on Daniel 3:1-28

Do a bit of model making: find the biggest cardboard box you can, and make it into a television or computer. Get the children to cut up some paper and make it into mock banknotes. If space permits, you could even use cartons to make a mock-up car. Use their imagination to think of other contemporary 'idols'.

• Think about the actions for all the children to join in during the story.

ON THE DAY

Introduction

We're going to think in a few minutes about some of the things people worship. First, we'll say our 'Thank you' Prayer.

'Thank you' Prayer

Thank you, God, for all you give us,
thank you for the earth and sea;
thank you, God, for special people,
thank you, God, for making me.

God's Story

This is a story about three men called Shadrach, Meshach and Abed-nego. They were slaves in Babylon. King Nebuchadnezzar realised they were very clever and thought they might be useful to him. So he gave them a fairly good life. As long as they didn't cause any trouble they would be well looked after.

Everything seemed to go very well, until the king got a little too big for his boots. He made a big golden statue, as tall as three houses put on top of one another. Why was it so big? Well, he just thought that bigger meant better, and he wanted to have the biggest statue around. Then, when he'd had it built he decided that it was so wonderful it must be a god, and he told everybody to worship it. That may seem a bit daft to you, but just be thankful they didn't have rock stars or footballers in those days or they might have worshipped something *really* silly . . .

Anyway, the king decided that he was going to have some fun. 'We're going to play musical prayers,' he said. 'As soon as the music starts, you've all got to lie down and pray. And anyone who isn't lying down by the time the music stops is out. *Permanently*! Do you understand what I mean?'

Some people weren't sure, so the king spelt it out for them. 'Anyone not praying to this wonderful god I've made will be thrown into the burning fiery furnace,' he explained. 'Is that clear enough for you?'

'I think I understand,' said a voice in the crowd. 'You mean we'll be out. *Permanently*.'

'Well done,' said the king. 'I do believe you've got it.'

Shadrach, Meshach and Abed-nego were among the crowd waiting for the music to start. Shadrach turned to his friends and said, 'I don't fancy the burning fiery furnace, but I don't want to worship that heap of scrap metal, either.'

'Neither do I,' said Meshach. 'It can't be a god – after all, it was made by people which seems just a little bit the wrong way round to me.'

'It's an ugly brute, anyway,' added Abed-nego. 'How can anyone worship anything as repulsive as that?'

Just then, the music started.

- the *trumpets were blown*,
- the *drums were beaten*,
- the *cymbals were crashed*

Everyone else lay down very quickly except Shadrach, Meshach and Abed-nego. 'Ooh, look!' cried the King's Personal Private Secretary, who was a really bloodthirsty person and quite mad. 'They're not bowing down! They're not worshipping! They're talking! Ooh, Your Majesty! Can I stoke the fire? Can I pour some oil on it? Go on, Your Majesty! Please let me pour some oil on it. Nasty little forriners – think they can come over here and do as they like! Please let me stoke the furnace, Your Majesty!'

'Oh, do shut up!' said the king, who was really tired of his secretary's silliness. Then he called out. 'Hey, you three. Didn't you hear the music?'

'Oh, yes – we heard it,' answered Shadrach, 'but if you think we're bowing down to that heap of scrap metal you've got another think coming – Your Majesty.'

The king was hopping mad, and his nasty little secretary was delighted.

'Ooh! Listen to that!' screamed the PPS. 'Put 'em in the fire, Your Majesty! Put 'em in the fire! That'll teach 'em a lesson – I'll bet they do as they're told after that! Go on, Your Majesty! Show 'em whose country this is!'

The king was very tempted to put his Personal Private Secretary on the fire as well, but he didn't. He didn't really want to do it to Shadrach, Meshach and Abed-nego either, because he liked them. 'Look, you chaps,' he said, 'why don't you just do it and save us all a lot of grief? You don't have to *mean* it. Just lie down and move your lips, and that will be enough.'

'No,' said Shadrach.

'Well, would you just kneel, then,' suggested the king.

'Not likely,' said Meshach.

'Just a quick bow? If we all close our eyes?' said the king desperately.

'Not on your life!' said Abed-nego.

The PPS was jumping up and down with excitement.

'Go on, Your Majesty. Burn 'em! Coming in here, bringing all their relations with them, eating our food, taking our jobs – put 'em on the fire, Your Majesty! Put 'em on the fire!'

So, very reluctantly, the king had to order that Shadrach, Meshach and Abed-nego be tied up and put into the furnace. The PPS had the time of his life, and he kept going to the spy-hole to peep in and see if they were burning. Suddenly he came running back towards the king.

'Your majesty!' he screeched, 'They're walking about. And none of them is burning! Tell 'em to burn, Your Majesty – tell 'em to burn!'

Immediately, the king had the furnace opened, and Shadrach, Meshach and Abed-nego came out. There wasn't so much as a scorched eyebrow between them. The king was thrilled to bits! 'We're not going to worship gold and silver any more,' he said. 'From now on we'll worship God.'

Our Story

Point out the models to the children. Are the various things evil in themselves? (We all need money, some of us actually need computers; and televisions and cars have a proper place in our lives. So when do they start to become idols?

Prayers

We're Glad

Thank you, God,
for giving us the things we need.
Help us to enjoy them,
but never to let them get so important
that we forget about you,
or about each other.

We're Sad

We're sorry, God,
for sometimes letting things
become more important than people.
Help us to value each other,
and especially people who are different
from us.

Let's Pray for People

We pray for people whose ideas are distorted
by money, or pride.
We pray for people who suffer prejudice
just because they're a little bit different.
Help us all to make the world a better
and kinder place for everyone in it.

Songs

Holy, holy, holy is the Lord
I'm black, I'm white, I'm short, I'm tall
Lord, the light of your love
You are the King of Glory

Walking Through Fire for God

God's Story

Narrator This is the story of Shadrach, Meshach and Abed-nego. They actually came from Jerusalem, but they had been taken to Babylon as slaves. The king was kind to them though, and life wasn't too bad until he got a little too big for his boots. He made a golden statue, and told everybody to worship it. That may seem a bit daft to you, but just be thankful they didn't have rock stars or footballers in those days or they might have worshipped something *really* silly . . .

King As soon as the music starts, you've all got to lie down and pray. And anyone who doesn't will end up in the fiery furnace.

Narrator Shadrach, Meshach and Abed-nego were among the crowd waiting for the music to start.

Shadrach I don't want to worship that monstrosity.

Meshach Neither do I. It can't be a god.

Abed-nego It's an ugly brute, anyway.

Shadrach Of course, beauty is in the eye of the beholder.

Abed-nego Who wrote that?

Shadrach No one yet, but someone famous will, one day.

Meshach I know! That's what some mindless hooligan scrawled on the warthog cage at the zoo.

Narrator Just then, the music started. Everyone lay down except Shadrach, Meshach and Abed-nego. The King's Personal Private Secretary, who was very bloodthirsty and quite mad, got really excited.

PPS Ooh, look! They're not bowing down! Ooh, Your Majesty! Can I stoke the fire? Nasty little forriners – think they can come here and do as they like! Please let me stoke the furnace, Your Majesty!

King	Do shut up! Hey, you three. Bow down and pray.
Shadrach	What, to that heap of scrap metal? Not likely!
Narrator	The king's Personal Private Secretary got excited.

- He *shovelled coal onto the fire,*
- he *fanned the flames,*
- and he *clapped his hands in delight*

PPS	Ooh! Listen to that! Put 'em in the fire, Your Majesty! Show 'em whose country this is! That'll teach 'em – I'll bet they do as they're told after that!
Narrator	The king was very tempted to put his Personal Private Secretary on the fire as well, but he didn't.
King	Look, you chaps, you don't have to *mean* it. Just lie down and move your lips, and that will be enough.
Shadrach	No.
King	Well, would you just kneel, then?
Meshach	Not likely!
King	Just a quick bow? If we all close our eyes?
Abed-nego	Not on your life!
PPS	Go on, Your Majesty. Burn 'em! Coming in here, bringing all their relations, eating our food, taking our jobs – put 'em on the fire, Your Majesty! Put 'em on the fire.
King	Oh, you are a pain! Still, you'd better do it.
Narrator	The PPS put the three men into the furnace, but suddenly he came running back towards the king.
PPS	Your Majesty! They're walking about. And none of them is burning! Tell 'em to burn, Your Majesty – tell 'em to burn!
Narrator	The king had the furnace opened, and Shadrach, Meshach and Abed-nego came out. There wasn't so much as a scorched eyebrow between them.
King	That's it. We're not going to worship gold and silver any more. From now on we'll worship God.

A Camel's Eye View

Based on Matthew 2:1-12

BEFORE THE DAY

Ask the children what they would like the world to be like. Suggest positive things: everyone cared for; food for everybody; peace, etc. Get the children to cut out star shapes from card, and write their hopes on them. Before the assembly, put them around the walls of the hall.

• Think about the actions for all the children to join in during the story.

ON THE DAY

Introduction

In a moment or two, we'll be hearing part of the Christmas story. First, we'll say our 'Thank you, prayer.

'Thank you' Prayer

Thank you, God, for all you give us,
thank you for the earth and sea,
thank you, God, for special people,
thank you, God, for making me.

God's Story

Let me introduce myself. My name's Constance, and I'm a camel. Not just any ordinary camel, mind you. I'm a Bactrian camel, which means I've got breeding. Straight out of the top drawer of four-legged Arabian society. I'm not prejudiced, though – some of my best friends are dromedaries. I fully realise that they can't help being different, and I've got nothing against them. Mind you, I wouldn't want one as an in-law, though – but that's another matter. I suppose I'd better get on with telling you the story. It's about the people who live in my annexe – Caspar, Balthazar and Melchior, otherwise known as the Three Wise Men.

It all began one evening when I was relaxing with my friend Clarissa, chewing away at some very tasty fig leaves. We were just saying that it seemed a lot lighter than usual at that time of night when the three wise men rushed in, all excited – without even knocking. Apparently there was a big star in the sky and they reckoned it meant a new king had been born. And they had Clarissa and me, and the other camels, harnessed up so fast I nearly choked on my fig leaf.

Soon, we were plodding across the desert, following this star. We had to travel by night, of course, so that we could see it, and rest in the day. When we worked out where we were going, I began to think something was seriously adrift. It looked to me as though we were heading for Judea. Now I wasn't happy about that; I'd heard about Judea from other camels I'd met on the trade routes. Apparently the people there weren't too keen on foreigners. More than that, they thought their God didn't approve of astrology, so I didn't think they'd exactly welcome us. Still, the wise men were urging us on and who was I to argue? Not that it would have done any good, anyway. Humans expect us to understand them, but they never seem to have a clue what we're saying! And they think they're a superior breed!

Anyway, to return to the story, we trailed across the desert following this star. My dears, it was simply frightful! We had to put up with sandstorms, flies and the most obnoxious little sand lizards who seemed to think they had as much right to be there as we did. Really! Then eventually, we saw the city of Jerusalem ahead, and stopped at the palace. At least that was a reasonable place for a quadruped of my breeding. Caspar decided to go and see the king.

• He *dusted himself down*
• He *straightened his coronet*
• and he *knocked on the palace door*

Soon, the king came out – chap called Herod. I don't mind telling you, I didn't like what I saw. Shifty character – couldn't look me straight in the eye. 'Hello, hello, hello,' I thought. 'He's a wrong 'un or I'm an African elephant.' Well, Herod didn't seem too pleased to hear that another king had been born – and I have to say I had some sympathy

– but after he'd done some checking up he sent us along the road to Bethlehem. He asked the wise men to go back when they'd found the baby king and tell him where he was 'so that he could pay his respects', he *said*. And if you believe that, then you will believe anything! Anyway, I wasn't happy about going to Bethlehem. Bethlehem, my dears, is one of those dreadful little tourist resorts where the common creatures go. Most of the humans ride donkeys – and some even walk! Would you believe it? I could have told Caspar, Melchior and Balthazar that they'd never find a king there. Still, they wouldn't listen – so off we set. My dears it was simply ghastly. There were great crowds of common people there, all pushing and jostling one another in the most vulgar way. Then the star stopped and shone down as if to say, 'This is the place'. Well, I always knew astrology was a very dubious business, and now it's been proved to me. You will simply never guess where it had led us. It was a stable. A horrid, smelly, draughty little hovel of a stable. And there, inside, was a baby and – my dears, you'll never guess – it was lying in a feeding trough, with the most disreputable ox I have ever seen breathing all over it. Then in went the three wise men – 'wise'? – I like that! And they brought out their presents. You should have seen what they gave the child. Gold – real solid twenty-two carat gold – none of your cheap plate – then some incense, and finally some spice – a particularly smelly variety called myrrh. And to think that all the way along I'd been blaming Clarissa's feet!

That night, I hardly got a wink of sleep. The three wise men were chattering away until the small hours – going on as though they'd had a ringside seat at the gladiators world cup final in Rome! I wanted to say to them, 'It's only a baby – you could have seen one of those at home,' but they wouldn't have listened. Then in the morning Caspar said a very strange thing. 'Let's give the palace a miss,' he said. 'An angel told me that Herod's not to be trusted.' Well, *I* could have told him that! Anyway, we went home by a different way – and a longer one – and Clarissa's feet haven't been right since.

What was it all about? My dears, don't ask me! One thing I do know, though: if it *does* turn out to be important it will be just like everything else. The camels do the walking, and the humans get all the credit.

Our Story

Point out the stars around the walls. Like the wise men, we too have to 'follow a star'. If the star is worth following it will always bring us into contact with people. And as long as we're not such terrible snobs as Constance and Clarissa were, we might actually enjoy it.

Prayers

We're Glad

Thank you, God, for giving us 'stars' to follow.
Thank you for the hopes and dreams we have about a better world, with more love,
more truth, more justice.
Help us to follow our dreams
as the wise men followed their star,
and to enjoy the people we meet on the way.

We're Sad

Sometimes, God, we don't follow.
It's easier to stay where we are,
where it's comfortable and safe
and nothing challenges us.
Forgive us for choosing the easy way,
and help us to follow you better.

Let's Pray for People

We pray for people whose lives are dull,
because they never had the chance
to dream or to hope.
We pray for people who *do* dream, and hope.
Please God, help us all to hope for a better
  world,
and to follow our star.

Songs

In the first stage of seeking
Lord, the light of your love
One more step along the world I go
We three kings of Orient are

A Camel's Eye View

God's Story

Narrator	My name's Constance, and I'm a camel – and before anyone says I've got the hump, let me tell them that that joke isn't funny any more. Or not to a camel of *my* breeding, anyway. I'm a *Bactrian* camel, which means I'm straight out of the top drawer of four-legged Arabian society, but this story's actually about the people who live in my annexe – Caspar, Balthazar and Melchior, otherwise known as the Three Wise Men. It all began one evening when I was relaxing with my friend Clarissa, chewing at some very tasty fig leaves.
Caspar	Melchior! Balthazar! Look!
Balthazar	That's some star! What d'you think, Melchior?
Melchior	That's the star of a new king. Saddle the camels.
Narrator	Well! We trailed across the desert following this star. My dears, it was simply frightful! We had to put up with sandstorms, flies and the most obnoxious little sand lizards who seemed to think they had as much right to be there as we did. Really! Eventually, we seemed to have arrived.

- Melchior *held up his hand*
- then he *peered into the distance*
- and then he *pointed with his finger*.

Melchior	There's the king's palace.
Narrator	That seemed a reasonable place for a quadruped of my breeding. Caspar knocked on the door.
Herod	Good evening, I'm King Herod. Can I help you?
Narrator	*(Aside)* Hello, hello, hello, he's a wrong 'un or I'm an African elephant.
Caspar	Hello, we're the three wise men.
Herod	How wonderful to meet you! I'm Herod the Great –

	but great what, I can never remember. Do come in – d'you take one lump or two?
Narrator	Smarmy character – wouldn't trust him an inch. Anyway, the wise men came out a little later, all excited.
Caspar	Well, who'd have thought it – Bethlehem.
Narrator	Oh, no! Bethlehem, my dears, is one of those dreadful little tourist resorts where the common creatures go. Most of the humans ride *donkeys* – and some even walk! Would you believe it?
Melchior	What a nice man Herod is – we must remember to tell him where the king is after we've found him.
Balthazar	Yes, then he can pay his respects, as well.
Narrator	Huh! If they believe that, then they'll believe anything!
Melchior	The star's stopped. This is the place.
Narrator	Well, the place confirmed my doubts about astrology. It was a horrid, smelly, draughty little hovel of a stable. And there, inside, was a baby and – my dears, you'll never guess – it was lying in a feeding trough, with the most disreputable ox I have ever seen breathing all over it. Then in went the three wise men – 'wise'? – I like that! And they offered their presents.
Melchior	I've brought the king some gold.
Caspar	And I've got some frankincense.
Balthazar	Here's some lovely myrrh.
Narrator	Ugh! Nasty, smelly stuff! And to think that all the way along I've been blaming Clarissa's feet! Anyway, next morning we got ready to leave.
Caspar	Let's give the palace a miss. An angel told me that Herod's not to be trusted.
Narrator	Well, I could have told him that! Anyway, we went home by a different way – and a longer one – and Clarissa's feet haven't been right since.

A Tale of Two Houses

Based on Matthew 7:24-27

BEFORE THE DAY

Get the children to do two jigsaw puzzles: one on a cloth, and the other on a solid tray.

• Think about the actions for all the children to join in during the story.

ON THE DAY

Introduction

Our class has done a jigsaw puzzle, and we're going to show it to you. First we'll say our 'Thank you' Prayer.

'Thank you' Prayer

Thank you, God, for all you give us,
thank you for the earth and sea;
thank you, God, for special people,
thank you, God, for making me.

Two children bring in the first puzzle, holding the cloth between them. What a shame. But it wasn't their fault it fell apart, was it? What was wrong?

God's Story

Jesus wanted to show his friends that although faith is sometimes hard, and needs a lot of patience, it's worth it in the end. So he told them a story a little like this one.

Sam and Joe were friends, but they were very different people. Sam was very patient and careful, whereas Joe was quite the opposite. 'Life's too short to worry about details,' he said one day, slapping another coat of paint on the fence.

'Maybe,' said Sam, 'but you've painted that fence twice this year. It would last longer if you rubbed it down first.'

One day, Sam decided to build himself a new house, elsewhere. 'Why don't you come with me?' he asked Joe. 'You could build yourself a new house as well.'

Joe thought that would be a wonderful adventure! They found and bought a piece of land between them, and started to build their houses. 'This is a good spot,' said Sam. 'The ground's nice and firm; let's start digging the foundations.'

It was hard work! Sam had chosen a very hard bit of ground indeed. Joe soon got fed up with digging in the hard rock and went off to a nice sandy patch where it was easier. Sam didn't think that was a good idea, but Joe had made up his mind and started digging in the sand. Very soon, he'd got the foundations dug and was starting to build his house. He'd got the walls nearly finished while Sam was still digging. By the time Sam started on his walls, Joe had got the roof on, and when Sam was working on his roof, Joe was sitting in a deckchair outside his front door, watching. 'I've finished,' he called out. 'I told you you should have built it over here on this nice soft sand.' Sam just kept on working and eventually his house was ready.

For a time, Sam and Joe were very happy in their houses, although Sam sometimes got fed up with Joe teasing him about being a slow coach. But all that changed on the night of the Great Storm.

It happened quite gradually at first. The wind began to get stronger, and started blowing the sand about. Joe and Sam weren't too worried; they just closed their doors and settled down to a quiet evening in their houses. Joe noticed his house swaying slightly, but he told himself it was probably good to have a little bit of 'give' in it.

Later, as Joe was getting into bed, Sam was looking out of his window thinking, 'I hope Joe's going to be all right – this storm's really getting going now.' Before very long, rain was rattling on the roofs of the houses, beating on the windows and making little pools on the ground outside.

Now, perhaps you've made sandcastles at the seaside, and seen what happens when the tide comes in and washes the sand away. Well, unfortunately, Joe had never made sandcastles, so he didn't know – but he was about to find out!

The first thing Joe knew was when he was woken by a loud creak. 'Hey up!' thought Joe (because he'd always secretly wanted to be a northerner, even though he wasn't – and he thought that northerners always said 'Hey up!') 'I think summat's up. Oh, well. It'll keep 'til t'morning.' (Actually, Joe had only ever been to the north once, and that was on holiday – so he had some very strange ideas!)

Joe could hear the wind and the rain outside, and kept telling himself that the way the house was swaying from side to side didn't matter. But it was frightening.

- He *pulled the covers over his head*
- and he *closed his eyes tightly*
- and suddenly he *jumped out of his skin.* Oh!

With an enormous 'crack!' the wall beside his bed had started to move, and before long there was a big gap in the corner with rain pouring in. Joe leapt out of bed, and rushed outside to see what had happened. All the sand around the base of the house had been washed away, and the whole house was moving and falling apart. In fact, it was lucky Joe had gone outside, because without any warning at all the roof went crashing down and landed right on the bed where he had been sleeping.

Well, there Joe was, out in the cold, wet, windy, outdoors wearing nothing but some very soggy pyjamas and an equally embarrassed look. Then he heard a voice. 'You'd better come into my place,' said Sam. 'I've got a nice warm fire going.'

'Ee, lad, that's reet good!' said Joe, and Sam smiled patiently because he actually was from the north, and he never spoke like that!

'You're welcome to stay until the storm blows over,' he said, 'and then we'll sort that house of yours.'

So in the morning they had a look at the wreckage, and Sam said, 'Actually, the house itself was a very good one; it just needed a better foundation – something really solid that could stand up to the storms. The trouble is that to put that right you'll have to start all over again.'

'Yes,' said Joe, who was a much wiser man now and had even dropped the phoney accent.

'I'll build it on the rock next time. It's worth the effort in the long run. Perhaps "instant everything" isn't such a good idea.'

Our Story

Bring in the other puzzle, on the tray. It might seem silly to have tried to carry the first one on that floppy cloth, but lots of people base their lives on things that are really no more substantial!

Prayers

We're Glad

Thank you, God,
for taking time with us.
Thank you for being patient
when we get things wrong,
and for working hard with us
to help us learn.

We're Sad

Sometimes we want good things
to happen instantly.
We want to be clever,
and have lots of good friends,
but we give up too soon
when things get difficult.
Help us to trust you and each other,
and to be willing to take time.

Let's Pray for People

Some people have to be patient,
especially with other people!
Please God, bless all those who care for others,
all those who try to help and heal;
and strengthen their faith
during the difficult times.

Songs

Abba, Father, let me be
Be the centre of my life
Don't build your house on the sandy land
Each of us is a living stone
The wise man built his house upon the rock

A Tale of Two Houses

God's Story

Narrator   Sam and Joe were friends, but they were very different people. Sam was very patient and careful, whereas Joe was quite the opposite.

Joe   Life's too short to worry about details.

Sam   Maybe, but you've painted that fence twice this year. It would last longer if you rubbed it down first. Actually, Joe, I've decided to build myself a new house somewhere else. Why don't you come with me? You could build yourself a new house as well.

Narrator   Joe thought that would be a wonderful adventure! They found and bought a piece of land between them, and began to build their houses.

Sam   This is a good spot. The ground's nice and firm; let's start digging the foundations.

Joe   No, it's too hard. I'll have this nice sandy bit over here. It's easier to dig.

Narrator   Joe got on quickly, and was soon sitting in a deckchair outside his front door, watching Sam work.

Joe   I've finished. I told you you should have built it over here on this soft sand.

Narrator   Sam just kept on working and eventually his house was ready. For a time, Sam and Joe were very happy in their houses, although Sam sometimes got fed up with Joe teasing him about being a slow coach. But all that changed on the night of the Great Storm. The rain rattled on the roofs of the houses, beating on the windows and making little pools on the ground outside. The first sign of trouble was when Joe was woken by a loud creak.

Joe   Hey up! I think summat's up. Oh, well. It'll keep 'til t'mornin'.

Narrator   Joe talked like that because he'd always secretly wanted to be a northerner, even though he wasn't. Actually, Joe had only ever been to the north once, and that was on holiday – so he had some very strange ideas! Joe could hear the wind and the rain outside, and kept telling himself that the way the house was swaying from side to side didn't matter. But it was frightening.

- He *pulled the covers over his head*
- and he *closed his eyes tightly*
- and suddenly he *jumped out of his skin*. Oh!

With an enormous 'crack!' the wall beside his bed had moved, and Joe got out just in the nick of time before the roof came crashing down and landed right on the bed where he had been sleeping. All the sand around the base of the house had been washed away, and the whole house was moving and falling apart. Joe heard a voice.

Sam   You'd better come into my place. I've got a nice warm fire going.

Joe   Ee, lad, that's reet good!

Narrator   Sam smiled patiently because he actually was from the north, and he never spoke like that! In the morning they had a look at the wreckage.

Sam   Actually, the house itself was a very good one; it just needed a better foundation – something really solid that could stand up to the storms. The trouble is that to put that right you'll have to start all over again.

Joe   Yes. I'll build it on the rock next time. It's worth the effort in the long run. Perhaps 'instant everything' isn't such a good idea.

The Fall of the Pharisee

Based on Matthew 12:9-14

BEFORE THE DAY

'Brainstorm' some rules with the children. First, what rules would they make if they wanted to make the world better (e.g. 'No stealing', 'No bullying', etc.) Then what if they were trying to make people unhappy? ('Don't visit Granny on Sundays', etc.) Write these on pieces of paper and put on display without saying which heading they come under.

* Think about the actions for all the children to join in during the story.

ON THE DAY

Introduction

We're going to hear a story about a lawyer who was so strict that he made everybody unhappy. First, we'll say our 'Thank you' Prayer.

'Thank you' Prayer

Thank you, God, for all you give us,
thank you for the earth and sea,
thank you, God, for special people,
thank you, God, for making me.

God's Story

Sam was doing very well for himself. He was a Pharisee, and that made him an important person in the town. Whenever he went out, he would put his fine robes on and everyone would move out of his way and say 'Good morning' very respectfully as he passed by. It was a wonderful life. Sam's legal practice was doing very well, too. People would come to see him to ask difficult questions, and he would look up his big law books to find out what they should do. He was very careful always to get it right; all the answers he needed were there in the books, and he would tell people, 'Do what the books say and you

can't go wrong. But if you don't do that, then God won't love you any more, and you know what that means, don't you?'

Of course, people always did what Sam said. From time to time he would get an awkward client who came back and said it hadn't worked, but Sam always found an answer. He could easily show that it was their fault in some way, and in thirty years he'd never once had to give anyone their fee back.

Then gradually people stopped coming to see him. It didn't take him long to find out why: someone had started up a rival practice. It turned out it was a man called Jesus who was going around giving advice without charging for it.

'That's unfair competition, that is,' thought Sam, and went along to listen to Jesus to find out more about him.

'Of course God still loves you,' Jesus was saying. 'God doesn't turn against you just because you've made a mistake.'

What? Could Sam really be hearing this? Why, if everyone went around saying God loved bad people, where would it end up?

'Now you know about that,' Jesus continued, 'you can stop being afraid of God and concentrate on loving him back.'

No wonder people weren't coming to Sam to pay high fees for hard advice, when they could hear nice things like that for nothing! And there was even a rumour that Jesus healed people who were sick, which Sam certainly couldn't compete with. Something had got to be done!

On the Sabbath, there was a newcomer in the synagogue. Sam particularly noticed the man because his right arm was paralysed. Suddenly, he had an idea. 'Hello,' he said, 'I don't think we've met. I'm Sam.'

'I'm Adam,' answered the other man. 'I'm on holiday here.'

'Well, don't stay at the back,' said Sam. 'Come and have a good seat right at the front.' And Sam put Adam right where he knew Jesus would see him.

It worked. Jesus came in and saw Adam's paralysed arm straight away. Sam watched, and thought, 'If he breaks the law by healing that man on the rest day, we've got him.'

Jesus knew what he was thinking. 'Tell me,

Sam,' he asked, 'if you had a cow that fell into a well on the Sabbath, would you leave it there?'

Oh, dear! Sam couldn't answer that. 'Well, um, I . . . that is . . . on the one hand . . . it all depends . . . on the other hand . . .'

By now, everyone in the synagogue was watching. The truth was that most people hated Sam because he was such a snob and because he always tried to make life as hard for them as he could. They'd never met anyone before who could win an argument against him, and they weren't going to miss out on the opportunity now!

As the crowd got bigger and more inquisitive, Sam got redder and more embarrassed. 'Come on, Sam,' shouted a bystander. 'What would you do?'

'He'd look up his books,' said one person.

'And give the cow some advice,' laughed another.

'And send it a bill!' added a third.

Sam had had enough. He drew himself up to his full height, pulled his Pharisee's robe close around himself, put on his most ferocious-yet-dignified-expression, and walked resolutely towards the door.

He got just a couple of metres before he bumped into someone. This was the first time he could ever remember people not moving out of his way. Something seemed to have changed around here, and it wasn't for the better!

It was no good; Sam just had to stay there and try to answer Jesus' question.

Jesus answered it for him. 'I know you would go and rescue that cow. Now, wouldn't you say that this man is just a little more important?' Then he turned to Adam. 'Stretch out your hand,' he said.

Adam didn't dare believe he'd be able to, in case he was disappointed. So he decided to work up to it gradually.

- First he just *wiggled a finger*
- Then he *clenched his fist*
- Then he *waved his arm over his head* for all he was worth!

No one was more amazed than Adam when he found that he could do that! 'I'm healed!' he said. 'Just wait until I tell my friends back home.'

There was a real celebration in the synagogue that day – mainly because everybody was happy for Adam. But there was another reason as well. From that day on, things were going to be different in that town.

Our Story

Ask the assembly what they think about the rules. Which are the healthy ones, and which are the silly ones? Might the silly ones have been made with good intentions? ('Don't visit Granny on Sunday' would cut road congestion!)

Prayers

We're Glad

Thank you, God,
for being who you are.
Thank you for being a loving parent,
not a fearsome judge.
Thank you for loving us
even when it hurts.

We're Sad

Sometimes, it's easier to threaten people
than to love them;
easier to try and force them to change
than to live with them as they are.
We're sorry, God,
if ever we've made you sound unloving to others.

Let's Pray for People

We pray for people who feel guilty,
who don't like themselves very much,
and think God doesn't like them either.
Please, God, help them to know you better
through the people they meet.
Fill us with your love, until it overflows
into the people around us.

Songs

God's love is deeper
Jesus' love is very wonderful
Let love be real
Make me a channel of your peace
There's a great big world out there

The Fall of the Pharisee

God's Story

Narrator	Sam was doing very well for himself. He was a Pharisee, and that made him an important person in the town. Whenever he went out, he would put his fine robes on and everyone would move out of his way. It was a wonderful life. Sam's legal practice was doing very well, too. People would come to see him to ask difficult questions, and he would look up his big law books to find out what they should do.
Sam	I'm very careful always to get it right; all the answers are there in the books. Do what they say and you can't go wrong. But if you don't do that, then God won't love you any more, and you know what that means, don't you?
Narrator	From time to time he would get an awkward client who came back and said the advice hadn't worked, but Sam could easily show that it was their fault in some way, and in thirty years he'd never once had to give anyone their fee back. Then gradually people stopped coming to see him. It seemed a man called Jesus was going around giving advice without charging for it. Sam went to listen to Jesus to find out more about him.
Jesus	Of course God doesn't turn against you just because you've made a mistake. So now you can stop being afraid of God and concentrate on loving him back.
Sam	What? Why, if the idea gets around that God loves bad people, where will it end up? I must do something!
Narrator	On the Sabbath, Sam got his chance. There was a newcomer in the synagogue. Sam particularly noticed the man because his right arm was paralysed.
Sam	Hello, I don't think we've met. I'm Sam.
Adam	I'm Adam. I'm on holiday here.
Sam	Well, don't stay at the back. Come and have a good seat right at the front.
Narrator	It worked. Jesus saw Adam straight away.

Sam	*(Aside)* If he heals that arm on the rest day, we've got him.
Jesus	Tell me, Sam, if you had a cow that fell into a well on the Sabbath, would you leave it there?
Sam	Well, um, I . . . that is . . . on the one hand . . . it all depends . . . on the other hand . . .
Narrator	By now, everyone in the synagogue was watching. The truth was that most people hated Sam because he was such a snob and because he always tried to make life as hard for them as he could. They'd never met anyone before who could win an argument against him, and they weren't going to miss out on the opportunity now!
1st Bystander	Come on, Sam. What would you do?
2nd Bystander	I know: he'd look up his books!
3rd Bystander	And give the cow some advice.
4th Bystander	And send it a bill!
Narrator	Sam had had enough. He pulled his Pharisee's robe close around himself and walked resolutely towards the door, but no one moved out of his way. Something seemed to have changed around here, and it wasn't for the better! Sam just had to stay there.
Jesus	I know you would go and rescue that cow. Now, wouldn't you say that this man is just a little more important? *(To Adam)* Stretch out your hand.
Narrator	Adam didn't dare believe he'd be able to.

- First he just *wiggled a finger*
- Then he *clenched his fist*
- Then he *waved his arm over his head* for all he was worth!

Adam	I'm healed! Just wait until I tell my friends back home.
Narrator	There was a real celebration in the synagogue that day – mainly because everybody was happy for Adam. But there was another reason as well. From that day on, things were going to be different in that town.

Roddy Raven's New Home

Based on Matthew 13:31

BEFORE THE DAY

Get the children to collect some seeds which they can stick on cards, perhaps with transparent tape, and to draw or paint the things that grow from them. You could also collect some actual examples, for example some tiny carrot seeds could be compared with some particularly large carrots, and so on.

• Think about the actions for all the children to join in during the story.

ON THE DAY

Introduction

They say, 'Little things mean a lot', and we're going to think about that in a minute. First, we'll say our 'Thank you' Prayer.

'Thank you' Prayer

Thank you, God, for all you give us,
thank you for the earth and sea,
thank you, God, for special people,
thank you, God, for making me.

God's Story

Hello, it's me: Roddy Raven. I've just got married to a rather wonderful bird called Rowena Rook. I've never been so happy since I was hatched. Rowena's so pleased she keeps on saying she wants us to have an egg, but I think we should wait. I mean, when we're settled I won't mind having a whole omelette, but you can't rush these things you know. And there was a time when I thought it was all going to go pear-shaped – if you'll excuse the metaphor. Let me tell you about it.

When Rowena said 'Yes', I thought everything was going to be wonderful. We went to see Ollie Owl to arrange the ceremony, and he suggested we might like to get some advice from the stork, but I told him that could wait. What we really wanted was a good choir; it turned out the Nightingales' Chorale were fully booked, so we had to make do with the Larks Philharmonic. Rowena's mum, Rachel, was disappointed but her dad *really* gave me a hard time.

'No daughter of mine,' said Ricky Rook, sternly, 'is getting married without somewhere decent to live.'

I said that our love would keep us warm, and he said I must be out of my tree. So I decided to get one.

I knew just the bird to talk to about finding a home. Cuthbert Cuckoo was an absolute genius at it. Some people said they weren't too happy about his methods, but I never pay attention to rumours.

'Now what d'you want?' Cuthbert asked me. 'I can fix you up with a nice little starter home on the Oaks Estate: hardly lived in, owners fell on hard times – know what I mean?'

I didn't know, and the way he was winking at me was irritating. 'Look,' I said, 'we're quite happy to build our own place; we just need a good site, really.'

'Build your own?' Cuthbert looked amazed. 'Why do that when I can get you one ready made? You find one you fancy and I'll get an eviction order. It'll be empty within the week.'

Now that I *really* didn't like the sound of. 'Just find us a good site,' I said. 'Leave the rest to us.'

Meanwhile, Ricky was getting really awkward. 'I hope you've found my daughter a home,' he squawked at me. Really, he's so old-fashioned! He seems to think that it's the male's job to sort everything out. I keep telling him, couples share everything these days, but he wouldn't listen.

'I'm not having my daughter marry a hippie,' he grumbled.

Hippie? What in the air is a hippie? Oh, never mind.

I must admit I was beginning to worry, myself. Eventually I decided to go and see how Cuthbert Cuckoo was getting on. I finally tracked him down by following the sound of squawking sparrows. Cuthbert was in the middle of enforcing an eviction order and seemed to be going a little over the top. So were the sparrows. When he'd finished I asked him, 'What about my home?'

Cuthbert frowned. 'The trouble is,' he said, 'there's been a real boom in the market recently, and all the best sites are already built on. I can find you a home ready built, but a vacant plot's really a problem.'

'Well you'd better sort it,' I said, 'because I'm getting fed up with all the hassle. How'd you like me to get the Fowl Play Commission to investigate your business methods?'

'You wouldn't!' he gasped.

'Try me!' I replied darkly. We ravens do most things darkly. And we certainly don't make threats lightly.

Well, as I expected, Cuthbert was round to see me within days. 'How long before your wedding?' he asked.

I told him and he seemed relieved. 'That's great,' he said. 'Come with me.'

Cuthbert took me to a big open field. There wasn't a decent tree in sight, and I was beginning to get impatient. Cuthbert pointed triumphantly. 'There!' he said.

All I could see was a man sowing seeds.

- He was *reaching into his bag*
- *holding up handfuls of seeds*
- and *scattering them all around*

'Never mind that,' Cuthbert insisted. 'What *kind* of seeds are they?' Now how on earth should I know that? Ravens are interested in food, not horticulture.

'They're *mustard* seeds,' said Cuthbert. 'And you know what mustard means?'

I hazarded a guess. 'Sausages?'

Cuthbert looked patient. 'By the time you're married, this field will be full of big bushes with enormous leaves. What better place for a couple of newlyweds to build their home?'

I looked at the seeds the farmer was sowing. They were tiny! 'Big bushes from those tiny seeds?' I shouted at Cuthbert. 'You must think I was hatched yesterday!'

'Wait and see,' Cuthbert pleaded. 'If I'm wrong, I'll take *myself* to the Fowl Play Commission. Fair enough?'

Well, he was right.

I was amazed.
Ricky was beaksmacked.
The wedding was wonderful.
And now everyone's happy.
Caw!

Our Story

Show the children the pictures/produce, and the seeds. You'll need to pass the cards around so that they can see them close up. Then help them to think about how little acts of kindness or of thoughtlessness can grow into big things like trust or resentment.

Prayers

We're Glad

Thank you, God, for your promise
that a little faith goes a long way.
Thank you for keeping us hopeful
when things are difficult,
and for giving us so much
in return for so little.

We're Sad

Sometimes, God, we don't notice
the 'little' things,
or we think that only big achievements matter.
Please help us to remember
that you can take even those things
that seem too small to be worthwhile,
and do something wonderful with them.

Let's Pray for People

Please, God, bless all the people
who think that their talents are too small.
Help them to value themselves,
to realise how much good you can do
with whatever they have to offer.
And help us to get our values
lined up with yours.

Songs

Push, little seed
This little light of mine
We eat the plants that grow from the seed
Who made the corn grow?

Roddy Raven's New Home

God's Story

Narrator*	Hello, it's me: Roddy Raven. I've just got married to a rather wonderful bird called Rowena Rook. She wants us to have an egg, but I think we should wait. I mean, when we're settled I won't mind having a whole omelette, but you can't rush these things you know. And there was a time when I thought it was all going to go pear-shaped – if you'll excuse the metaphor. Rowena's dad, Ricky Rook, *really* gave me a hard time.
Ricky	No daughter of mine is getting married without somewhere decent to live.
Roddy	Our love will keep us warm.
Ricky	You must be out of your tree!
Roddy	Well, I'm *trying* to get one!
Narrator	Mind you, he had a point. And I knew just the bird to talk to about finding a home. Cuthbert Cuckoo.
Cuthbert	Now what d'you want? I can fix you up with a nice little starter home on the Oaks Estate: hardly lived in, owners fell on hard times – know what I mean?
Roddy	Look, we're quite happy to build our own place; we just need a good site, really.
Cuthbert	Build your own? Why do that when I can get you one ready made? You find one you fancy and I'll get an eviction order. It'll be empty within the week.
Roddy	Now that I really don't like the sound of. Just find us a good site and leave the rest to us.
Narrator	Meanwhile, Ricky was getting really awkward.
Ricky	I hope you've found my daughter a home.
Roddy	Don't be so old-fashioned! I keep telling you, couples share responsibilities these days.

* Roddy and narrator are the same person. As 'Roddy' he engages in the dialogue with other characters; as 'Narrator' he addresses the audience.

Ricky   I'm not having my daughter marry a hippie.

Roddy   Hippie? What in the air is a hippie? Oh, never mind.

Narrator   Eventually I decided to go and see how Cuthbert Cuckoo was getting on. I tracked him down by the sound of squawking sparrows. Cuthbert was enforcing an eviction order and seemed to be going a little over the top. So were the sparrows.

Roddy   What about my home?

Cuthbert   I can find you a home ready built, but a vacant plot's really a problem.

Roddy   Well you'd better sort it, because I'm getting fed up. How'd you like me to get the Fowl Play Commission to investigate your business methods?

Narrator   As I expected, Cuthbert was round to see me within days. He took me to a big open field. There wasn't a decent tree in sight. All I could see was a man sowing seeds, and I was beginning to get impatient.

- The man was *reaching into his bag*
- *holding up handfuls of seeds*
- and *scattering them all around*

Cuthbert   They're *mustard* seeds, and what does that mean?

Roddy   Um . . . sausages?

Cuthbert   By the time you're married, this field will be full of big bushes with enormous leaves. What better place for a couple of newlyweds to build their home?

Roddy   Big bushes from those tiny seeds? You must think I was hatched yesterday!

Cuthbert   Wait and see. If I'm wrong, I'll take *myself* to the Fowl Play Commission. Fair enough?

Narrator   Well, he was right. I was amazed. Ricky was beak-smacked. The wedding was wonderful. And now everyone's happy. Caw!

Peter Gets His Feet Wet

Based on Matthew 14:22-33

BEFORE THE DAY

Suppose you wanted to distract someone and make concentration difficult: what sort of things might you do and say? Ask the children to write down some things that they might call out: 'Ooh, look – there's an elephant!' or 'Isn't that . . .*?' Check that they're usable, and then tell them to bring their papers to the assembly.

• Think about the actions for all the children to join in during the story.

ON THE DAY

Introduction

Now, here's a story about something you *definitely* shouldn't try for yourself! Before we hear it, though, we'll say our 'Thank you' Prayer.

'Thank you' Prayer

Thank you, God, for all you give us,
thank you for the earth and sea;
thank you, God, for special people,
thank you, God, for making me.

God's Story

After Jesus had fed the five thousand people, he and his disciples were very tired. 'I think it's time we got away,' said Jesus. 'Peter looks about done in.'

'Who? Me?' yawned Peter. 'I'm not tired.'

'I don't know what makes you think you're going to get away,' said Philip. 'This crowd's determined to make you king, and they're not going to be fobbed off.'

'I think you're right,' said Jesus. 'You all go home, and I'll follow you later. It's me they want, so as long as I'm here they won't follow you, and then I can slip away quietly.'

'You're not thinking, Jesus,' said Peter. 'If we've taken the boat, how are you going to get across the lake?'

'I imagine I'll think of something,' said Jesus, 'but if you all hang around with me none of us will get away.'

'He's right, you know,' said Thomas. 'Look, I vote we do as he says. He's a pretty resourceful chap and we ought to trust him more.'

So while Jesus held the crowd's attention, the disciples slipped quietly away and put out to sea where they watched for Jesus' signal to pick him up. But when Jesus had persuaded the crowd to go home, he went off to a quiet place on his own to pray. He had had people around him all day long and even Jesus found it difficult to listen to God properly in a crowd.

Meanwhile, the disciples were getting worried. They were well away from the shore, and a storm was threatening.

'Let's go back and find him,' suggested Matthew.

'He won't like that one little bit,' said James. 'You know he hates being fussed over, and he always seems to get by.'

'Well,' said John, 'we've got to do one or the other. We either go back or we go home, but if we stay here we're going to be caught in that storm that's brewing up.'

'That's it,' said Andrew, whose boat it was. 'We're going home. That's what Jesus told us to do, and anyway he's probably found somewhere to shelter for the night. We can come back for him in the morning, after the storm's over.'

So up went the sail, and before long the boat was cutting through the water towards Galilee.

Just as they thought they were going to make it, the wind changed and the water around the boat started thrashing violently.

• It *rocked to the left*
• it *rocked to the right*
• and it *rocked backwards and forwards*

For hours and hours, they battled to keep the ship afloat, but it seemed to be useless. Then, in the early hours of the morning, Andrew saw something that really made his hair stand on end. He nudged James and said, 'L-l-look over there.' When James looked he forgot about the storm and just stood staring with his mouth wide open.

'Hey!' bellowed Peter. 'Don't leave all the work to us.'

---

* The name of a favourite pop star or personality.

James just raised his hand and pointed a very shaky finger indeed back towards the shore they had come from. Peter looked where James was pointing and what d'you think he saw? He saw a man – not standing on the shore but walking towards them on the top of the water. He couldn't believe his eyes. Not only was it impossible then; it's still impossible even now!

After a few moments Andrew found his voice. 'It's a ghost!' he said. 'And it's after us.'

The 'ghost' called out. 'Don't be afraid. It's me – Jesus.'

'Oh, my life! It speaks as well!' wailed Andrew, who hadn't listened properly to what Jesus said.

Peter had heard clearly, though. 'Is that really you?' he called out. 'If it is, can I come and meet you?'

'Of course you can,' answered Jesus. 'Just keep your eyes on me and you'll be all right.'

Now, anyone else would have stepped out very carefully onto that raging sea – if they'd done it at all – but not Peter. He just climbed up on the side of the boat and jumped. And sure enough, he stayed on the top, just like Jesus. He took a few steps toward Jesus, and found that he could keep his balance quite easily although the sea was still pounding up and down. Then he got a bit silly.

'Hey, fellas! Look at me!' he called, turning round to look at his friends, 'It's easy! It's Ahh! Oh!! HEEEEEELP!'

Peter went right under the water. All his friends were very frightened, but Jesus just hurried over, reached out his hand and pulled Peter back to the surface again. 'Why won't you ever listen to me, and do as I say!' he exclaimed. 'I told you to keep looking at me – not start showing off to your friends. Come on, let's get you into the boat.'

As soon as they got into the boat, the storm stopped. Just like that!

It was then that the disciples realised that Jesus was no ordinary man, and they worshipped him. And not only they but all their neighbours started to recognise him and brought sick people to be healed by him.

As for Peter, he said he'd learnt his lesson. 'From now on', he said, 'I'll always trust him in a crisis, and stick with him.'

He meant it, too. He found out later that it wasn't that easy, but he came through in the end. He found that keeping his eye on Jesus didn't always make life easy for him – but it certainly made it interesting!

Our Story

Call the leading group out to the front, and set the rest of the assembly some mental task, e.g. 'What's 23 x 16?' While they're trying to work it out, get the children to read out their sentences at random, gradually getting louder and faster so that they're all shouting at once.

You can then explain that that was the kind of 'storm' life can sometimes become, and we find it difficult to concentrate on what's really important.

Prayers

We're Glad

Thank you, God,
for a world so full of excitement:
so much to do and see,
so many things to enjoy.
Thank you, God,
for this wonderful world.

We're Sad

Please forgive us, God,
when we become so distracted
that we forget what life's really about.
Help us to keep our eyes on you,
and not to get swamped by other things.

Let's Pray for People

We pray for people whose lives are busy;
who have lots of pressures on them.
Help them to keep their attention
on the things that are really important.

Songs

Do not be afraid
Father, I place into your hands
I danced in the morning
Make me a channel of your peace.

Peter Gets His Feet Wet

God's Story

Narrator After Jesus had fed the five thousand people, he and his disciples were very tired.

Jesus I think it's time we got away. You take the others home, Peter, and I'll follow you later when I've got rid of the crowd.

Peter You're not thinking, Jesus. If we've taken the boat, how are you going to get across the lake?

Jesus I imagine I'll think of something. If we all go at once, the crowd will follow. So get going, and I'll slip away and catch you up later.

Narrator So while Jesus held the crowd's attention, the disciples slipped quietly away and put out to sea where they watched for Jesus' signal to pick him up. But Jesus went off to a quiet place on his own to pray. He had had people around him all day long and even Jesus found it difficult to listen to God properly in a crowd. Meanwhile, Matthew was getting worried. They were well away from the shore, and a storm was threatening.

Matthew Let's go back and find him.

Peter He won't like that one little bit. You know he hates being fussed over, and he always seems to get by.

Matthew Well, we've either got to go back or go home, but if we stay here we're going to be caught in that storm that's brewing up. What d'you think, Andrew?

Andrew Let's go home. Jesus has probably found somewhere to shelter for the night. We can come back for him in the morning, after the storm's over.

Narrator So up went the sail, and before long the boat was cutting through the water towards Galilee. Just as they thought they were going to make it, the wind changed and the water around the boat started thrashing violently.

- It *rocked to the left*
- it *rocked to the right*
- and it *rocked backwards and forwards*

Suddenly, Andrew saw something that really made his hair stand on end.

Andrew   L-l-look, Peter. Someone's walking on the water.

Peter   It's a ghost! And it's after us.

Jesus   Don't be afraid. It's me – Jesus.

Peter   Is that really you? If it is, can I come and meet you?

Jesus   Of course you can. Just keep your eyes on me and you'll be all right.

Narrator   Now, anyone else would have stepped out very carefully onto that raging sea – if they'd done it at all – but not Peter. He just climbed up on the side of the boat and jumped. And sure enough, he stayed on the top, just like Jesus. He took a few steps, but then he got a bit silly.

Peter   Hey, fellas! Look at me! It's easy! It's Ahh! Oh!! HEEEEEELP!

Narrator   Peter went right under the water. Jesus just hurried over, reached out his hand and pulled Peter back to the surface again.

Jesus   Why won't you ever listen to me, and do as I say! I told you to keep looking at me – not start showing off to your friends. Come on, let's get you into the boat.

Peter   I've learnt my lesson. From now on, I'll always trust you in a crisis, and stick with you.

Funny Things, Mountains

Based on Matthew 17:1-9

BEFORE THE DAY

Ask the children to write or draw about their favourite activities. Hopefully, there will be a mixture of active/exciting things and more passive, relaxing activities. (If not, you might need to do a little persuasion!) Make a display of the pictures and writings.

• Think about the actions for all the children to join in during the story.

ON THE DAY

Introduction

We all need some excitement in our lives, and friends of Jesus are no exception. Before we think more about that, we're going to say our 'Thank you' Prayer.

'Thank you' Prayer

Thank you, God, for all you give us,
thank you for the earth and sea;
thank you, God, for special people,
thank you, God, for making me.

God's Story

Peter, James and John were finding it hard to keep up with Jesus.

'I must say,' James gasped, 'when Jesus said, "Follow me," I didn't think he meant up a mountain.'

'He's right, you know,' John agreed. 'No one ever said anything about a mountain.'

'I'm a sea-level man, myself,' puffed Peter. 'You know where you are with the sea. Funny things, mountains.'

Jesus stopped and waited for them to catch up. 'What are you so puzzled about?' he asked. 'Have you forgotten how important mountains are in our faith?'

John looked blank for a moment. 'I suppose

he might be thinking of Mount Sinai,' he said, as Jesus once again strode on ahead of them. 'That's where Moses received the law.'

'That's right!' James joined in. 'And then there was Mount Carmel, where Elijah had his showdown with the prophets of Baal. D'you think something important's going to happen on *this* mountain?'

'You've been reading too many books!' growled Peter. 'My brother went up a mountain once and it really turned his head. He came back with some cock and bull story about finding the remains of an ancient ship up there. Now, I ask you: what would a ship be doing up a mountain?'*

James and John looked at one another and shrugged.

'See what I mean?' said Peter, triumphantly. 'Funny things, mountains.'

By now, they were at the top. They flopped down on the grass and tried to get their breath back. The fact that Jesus still seemed so fresh and fit did nothing to make them feel any better!

'Look at him!' exclaimed James. 'He hasn't even broken sweat!'

'Yes, he has,' retorted Peter. 'Look how his face is shining.'

That was certainly true. It wasn't just his face that was shining, though, but all of him. His clothes looked like something out of a TV advert for washing powder (but of course, they hadn't invented washing powder then). The three disciples started getting uneasy. And they didn't feel any better when two other men appeared out of thin air.

• Peter *blinked*
• Then he *stared*
• and then he *scratched his head*

'Where'd they come from?' he demanded.

'Must've followed us up,' suggested John.

'No, they didn't. I'm not so tired I wouldn't have noticed someone following us,' Peter asserted.

It did seem strange. Who were these men? They looked terribly important, and Jesus was so engrossed in talking to them that he seemed to have forgotten all about his friends.

---

* Can you tell him? (If not, try Genesis 8:4.)

Suddenly, Peter had a very strange thought.

'You know what you two were saying on the way up – about Moses and Elijah? You don't suppose it's . . . can't be, can it? Just a thought.'

'Now who's been reading too many books?' demanded James.

'I think he's onto something,' said John. 'Think about it. Our Rabbi's always going on about the law and the prophets, isn't he?'

'How are you spelling profits?' asked Peter.

'You know perfectly well,' John answered sternly. 'Look, here's Jesus, with Moses and Elijah. The law and the prophets. Everything that's really important in our faith, all brought to completion in Jesus.'

'You're right!' Peter exploded, excitedly. 'Isn't it wonderful! We're the only ones to see this. Now we know that what we've been thinking about Jesus is true. Well, this is the stuff that religion's really about! Never mind all those prayers and sermons and things. I feel terrific!'

The others felt the same way. They were full of joy and exhilaration; their heads felt light, and it seemed as though the whole universe was shining with God's glory.

'Why can't it be like this all the time?' James mused.

'Why shouldn't it be?' Peter asked. 'Hey, Jesus! How about building some huts here. We could build three: one for you, one for Moses and one for Elijah. We need never go back down to that dull, mundane world again! Well, what d'you say?'

Before Jesus could answer, things took a very funny turn indeed. A dark cloud came over the mountain, and darkened everything – except Jesus who was still lit up like a lighthouse on a foggy night. As if that wasn't enough, a voice came from nowhere. 'This is my Son,' the voice thundered. 'I love him, and I want you to listen to him.'

By now, the three disciples had done what anyone with any sense would have done: hit the deck. After the voice, everything was eerily quiet, and eventually Peter dared to look up. Slowly opening his eyes, he was half-relieved and half-disappointed to find that everything seemed normal again. Jesus was by himself; no sign of the other two, and the Voice seemed to have said all it wanted to say, as well. 'Come on,' said Jesus, kindly. 'We've got to go back down again, now.'

No one was arguing with that, but Peter did get teased a little on the way.

'What was that about wanting to stay up there for ever?' laughed John.

'Let's just say I got carried away a bit,' replied Peter. 'It's like I told you. Funny things, mountains.'

Our Story

Draw attention to the display. Life's really exciting at times, isn't it? But we enjoy the less exciting parts of it, too. And that's just how God wants it to be.

Prayers

We're Glad

Thank you, God,
for the exciting moments.
Thank you for times of great happiness;
times when we feel so sure of you.
Thank you for being with us
in the ordinary things, as well.

We're Sad

Sometimes we get bored too easily, Jesus.
We want you to entertain us.
Help us to enjoy the high points,
but stop us from getting so high
that we can't see the earth any more!

Let's Pray for People

Loving God, please bless those people
for whom life is never exciting.
And when we're full of joy and enthusiasm,
help us to be sensitive to them, as well.

Songs

Give me joy in my heart
I danced in the morning
Jesus put this song into our hearts
One more step

Funny Things, Mountains

God's Story

Narrator	James and his friends were finding it hard to keep up with Jesus.
James	You know, Peter, when Jesus said, 'Follow me,' I didn't think he meant up a mountain. Did you, John?
John	No. No one ever said anything about a mountain.
Peter	I'm a sea-level man, myself. Funny things, mountains.
Narrator	Jesus stopped and waited for them to catch up.
Jesus	What are you so puzzled about? Have you forgotten how important mountains are in our faith?
John	I suppose he might be thinking of Mount Sinai. That's where Moses received the law.
James	That's right! And then there was Mount Carmel, where Elijah defeated the prophets of Baal. Perhaps something special's going to happen on *this* mountain.
Peter	You've been reading too many books!
Narrator	By now, they were at the top. They flopped down on the grass and tried to get their breath back.
James	Look at Jesus! He hasn't even broken sweat!
Peter	Yes he has. Look how his face is shining.
Narrator	That was certainly true. In fact, all of him was shining. Suddenly, two other men appeared out of thin air. • Peter *blinked* • Then he *stared* • and then he *scratched his head*
Peter	Where'd they come from?
John	Must've followed us up.

Peter	No, they didn't. I'm not *that* tired. I'd have noticed.
Narrator	The men looked terribly important, and Jesus was completely engrossed in talking to them.
Peter	You know what you two were saying on the way up – about Moses and Elijah? Could they be . . .?
James	Now who's been reading too many books?
John	I think he's onto something. Think about it. The Rabbis are always going on about the law and the prophets.
Peter	How are you spelling profits?
John	Look, here's Jesus, with Moses and Elijah. The law and the prophets. Everything that's really important in our faith, all brought to completion in Jesus.
Peter	You're right! Well, this is the stuff that religion's really about! It's exciting – spectacular! I feel terrific!
James	Why can't it be like this all the time?
Peter	Why shouldn't it be? Hey, Jesus! How about building three huts here for you, Moses and Elijah? We need never go back down to that dull world again!
Narrator	Before Jesus could answer, things took a very funny turn indeed. A dark cloud came over the mountain, and darkened everything – except Jesus. Then a voice came from nowhere.
God	This is my Son. I love him. Listen to him.
Narrator	By now, the three disciples were flat on their faces. After the voice, everything was eerily quiet, and eventually Peter dared to look up. Everything seemed normal again.
Jesus	Come on, we've got to go back down again, now.
Peter	I can't wait!
John	What was that about wanting to stay up there for ever?
Peter	Let's just say I got carried away a bit. It's like I told you. Funny things, mountains.

The Greatest

Based on Matthew 18:1-7

Ask the children who they think of as really 'great' people. Get them to cut out pictures from magazines, newspapers, etc. Fix them to a board, leaving a gap in the middle.

• Think about the actions for all the children to join in during the story.

ON THE DAY

Introduction

We're going to think about some really great people in a moment. First, we'll say our 'Thank you' Prayer.

'Thank you' Prayer

Thank you, God, for all you give us,
thank you for the earth and sea;
thank you, God, for special people,
thank you, God, for making me.

God's Story

Barney's mum and dad were talking about Important Matters. And that meant Barney wasn't included in the conversation, but he was used to that. Whenever there was anything interesting happening, he got left out. His parents were always very kind about it.

'One day, you'll be a man,' his father explained. 'Then you'll understand and be able to join in.'

'But how will I understand when I'm grown up if I don't get a chance to learn?' he asked.

Dad smiled in that annoying way parents have when they don't want children to know they're stuck for an answer. 'You'll understand when you're older,' he asserted, and went back to his Serious Conversation with Mum.

'I still think we should book Tuney Tim,' said Mum. 'Sally and James said he was wonderful at little Tom's party; he sang some lovely songs.

'Maybe,' replied Dad, 'but I've heard Mystery Mick the conjuror is really great. They had him next door for Rachel's tenth birthday. I think he'd be just right for Barney.'

'Well, I think . . .' Barney started to say.

'Not now, Barney, dear,' said Mum in her special patronising voice. 'Daddy and Mummy are very busy planning your lovely party, so why not just play with your nice little toys and let us get on with it.'

Barney cringed. When were they going to stop treating him like a baby? And whose party was it anyway?

Dad gave him another of those smiles and said, 'Mummy and Daddy know what's best.'

That, Barney told himself, was what *they* thought. He knew all about Tuney Tim. Most of his friends had had him for their party recently, because all the mums and dads loved him. Well, of course they would, wouldn't they? He was the same age as them, and he sang all the silly nursery rhymes they remembered. And as for that conjuror! *Everyone* knew how all those old tricks were done, but the parents thought the children were being fooled by it! Barney and his friends knew exactly what was going on, of course: their parties were being hijacked so that parents who were sorry they'd ever grown up could pretend to be children again – and it wasn't fair!

Just as Barney was wondering what to do, the mum from next door came bursting in, all excited. 'Guess what!' she said. 'Jesus is here. He's holding a meeting just up the hill.'

Mum and Dad jumped up as though they'd been stung. 'Jesus?' echoed Dad. 'We've got to go and hear him. Barney: Boots!'

'Oh, great!' thought Barney, grimly. 'What's he, a juggler or something?' But he knew it was no good arguing with his parents because they'd only say that They Knew Best. So he put his boots on and went out with them.

When they got to the place, he saw a man standing apart from the rest and talking to the crowd that was gathering. It was worse than a juggler: it was a preacher! This was one time Barney didn't mind when his parents told him to stay at the edge of the crowd. 'You can play with all your nice little friends,' Mum cooed. 'Won't that be lovely!' And Barney was put in a group of children being cared for by a fifty-five-year-old child with a bad memory.

Barney was just thinking how boring this was when he heard voices being raised. People were getting cross with each other, and that usually meant something interesting was going to happen. So Barney pricked up his ears. He recognised his dad's voice.

'All this is all very well, Jesus, but the point is who're the *really important* people going to be, when you're in power?'

Trust Dad. Always on about importance and power! Barney was about to look away again when he heard Jesus say, 'Bring me one of those children.'

'Oh dear,' thought Barney, 'another entertainer. What's it going to be: "Pick a card" or "What's that in your ear"? Barney had had so many strange objects fished out of his ear by magicians it was getting seriously boring, and he knew they really had them in their hands the whole time. The trick was always to watch the hand they were trying to distract you from. Barney wondered what child would be chosen.

- He *looked all around*
- then he *covered up his face* with his hands
- then he *peeked through his fingers*

But it was no use. To his horror, Barney found himself being grasped by the arm and dragged out to the front. 'Mustn't keep Jesus waiting!' muttered Dad. 'He's an Important Person.' And suddenly, Barney was standing in the middle of the crowd.

'Here's one of the most important people in God's world,' said Jesus. Barney looked around to see who Jesus meant, but everyone else was looking back at him! Jesus continued, 'God's not interested in cleverness, but in faith and humility. This is what you've all got to be like if you want to be Really Important. Now, why are all those children being kept out?' Suddenly, Jesus was surrounded by children, of all ages, and Barney found himself being talked to like a ten-year-old instead of a baby! But more importantly than that, Jesus *listened* to them just as carefully. He really seemed to be interested in what each child thought. And he never said, 'You're Too Young To Understand,' once!

All too soon, it was time to go, but Barney had an idea. 'Please Jesus,' he said, 'will you come to my birthday party?'

'Of course, I will!' replied Jesus. 'It's an honour to be invited.' He turned to Barney's parents. 'Will that be all right?'

Dad smiled. 'I wouldn't dare say no!' he answered. 'But you'd better come home, Barney. We're going to need your help to choose the best kind of food.'

Our Story

Look at the display of great people, and see if the wider group can identify them, and say why they're great. Then ask who is missing from the centre. Take a large felt marker pen and write 'YOU'. And why are *they* great? Because Jesus says so!

Prayers

We're Glad

Thank you, God,
for giving us two ears
to every one mouth!
Help us to listen to each other
and to share the wisdom
you have given us.

We're Sad

Very often we only see things
from our point of view.
So we don't see the complete picture,
but we act as if we did.
Forgive us, please, God,
and help us to help each other
understand things better.

Let's Pray for People

We pray for parents and children
who don't understand one another,
and who are unhappy.
Please, God, help all adults and children
to love each other the way you love them.

Songs

Father welcomes all his children
He's got the whole world in his hand
I'm black, I'm white, I'm short, I'm tall
Stand up! Walk tall

The Greatest

God's Story

Narrator	Barney's mum and dad were talking about Important Matters. And that meant Barney wasn't included in the conversation, but he was used to that.
Dad	One day, you'll be a man. Then you'll be able to join in.
Barney	But how, if I don't get a chance to learn?
Dad	You're too young to understand. Now, where were we?
Mum	I still think we should book Tuney Tim. Sally and James said he was wonderful at little Tom's party; he sang some lovely songs.
Dad	Maybe, but I've heard Mystery Mick the conjuror was great at next door's party. Barney would love him.
Barney	Well, I think . . .
Mum	Not now, Barney, dear. Daddy and Mummy are very busy planning your lovely party, so why not just play with your nice little toys and let us get on with it.
Narrator	Barney cringed. Dad gave him another of those smiles.
Dad	Mummy and Daddy know what's best.
Barney	*(Aside) That* is what *they* think.
Narrator	Barney knew all about Tuney Tim. All the mums and dads loved him. Well, of course they would, wouldn't they? He was the same age as them, and he sang all the silly nursery rhymes they remembered. And as for that conjuror, well! Barney and his friends knew exactly what was going on, of course: their parties were being hijacked so that parents who were sorry they'd ever grown up could pretend to be children again – and it wasn't fair! Just as Barney was wondering what to do, the mum from next door came bursting in, all excited.
Mum 2	Guess what! Jesus is here. He's just up the hill.

Narrator	Mum and Dad jumped up as though they'd been stung.
Dad	Jesus? We've got to go and hear him. Barney: Boots!
Barney	(*Aside*) Oh, great! What's he, a juggler or something?
Narrator	But Barney knew it was no good arguing with his parents because they'd only say that They Knew Best. So he put his boots on and went out with them. Oh, no! It was worse than a juggler: it was a preacher! This was one time Barney didn't mind when his parents told him to stay at the edge of the crowd.
Mum	You can play with all your nice little friends.
Narrator	Barney was just thinking how boring this was when he heard voices being raised. Barney pricked up his ears. He recognised his dad's voice.
Dad	All this is all very well, Jesus, but who're the *really important* people going to be, when you're in power?
Jesus	Bring me one of those children.
Barney	(*Aside*) Oh dear, I hope they don't choose me.
Narrator	• Barney *looked all around* • then he *covered up his face* with his hands • then he *peeked through his fingers*
Dad	Come on, Barney – mustn't keep Jesus waiting, he's an Important Person.
Jesus	Now, here's one of the most important people in God's world. Why are all the children being kept out?
Narrator	Suddenly, Jesus was surrounded by children. He really seemed to be interested in what they thought. And he never said, 'You're Too Young To Understand,' once!
Barney	Please Jesus, will you come to my birthday party?
Jesus	It's an honour to be invited. Will that be all right?
Dad	(*Smiling*) I wouldn't dare say no! But you'd better come home, Barney. We're going to need your help to choose the best kind of food.

Will He or Won't He?

Based on Matthew 21:28-32

BEFORE THE DAY

Ask the children to imagine they'd promised to do a job (such as tidying their room) and then broken their promise. Now of course we all know they wouldn't be untruthful . . . but can they imagine the kind of excuses some people might make. Write down some of these (especially the more outlandish ones) to post up in the assembly room.

• Think about the actions for all the children to join in during the story.

ON THE DAY

Introduction

We're going to think about broken promises today. First, we'll say our 'Thank you' Prayer.

'Thank you' Prayer

Thank you, God, for all you give us,
thank you for the earth and sea,
thank you, God, for special people,
thank you, God, for making me.

God's Story

Jonathan was looking forward to a day off. He worked with his father and brother on the family farm, and things had been really busy as they tried to get the harvest in on time. Today, though, was going to be different. He'd been promising himself a day out in the town for months and he knew they could manage without him for one day. After all, they'd only got a corner of one field left to do and there was plenty of time before the rains came.

So Jonathan wasn't pleased when his father came to him that morning and said, 'Just one more big push today and we'll have it done. I'd like you to get started in the field as soon as you can. I'll stay here and get the barn ready, so we can get the corn stored properly.'

Jonathan really wanted to help; he hated letting his father down. But there again, shouldn't he have a life of his own, at his age? 'If I'm old enough to work on the farm,' he said, 'I'm old enough to please myself. I'm going out.' And off he went.

Dad was terribly worried. 'If we don't get this last field done in time, we could be ruined!' he said. 'Ben, would you mind doing it?'

'Of course, Dad – no problem!' said Ben. 'Don't worry, I'm not selfish like Jonathan. You can rely on me.' And he set off for the farm.

On the way to the farm, he met Rebecca, the daughter of the farmer next door. 'Hi, Ben,' she called, brightly. 'Fancy going for a picnic?'

'I'd love to,' Ben answered sadly, 'but I've got to go and do some work in the fields.'

'Oh, that's a shame!' said Rebecca. 'It would have been so nice – just the two of us.'

Ben looked at Rebecca, and kept thinking, 'Just the two of us . . .' He'd never been able to talk to Rebecca without other people hearing, before. And the chance of being alone with her might not come again. There again, if Jonathan could please himself, he reasoned, why shouldn't he? The more he thought about it, the more angry he got with his brother. Jonathan was going to have a wonderful day out with his friend while *he* would have to work in the fields and miss the chance of a picnic with Rebecca.

'Why should I work, if Jonathan isn't!' he exploded. 'Come on, Rebecca; I hope you've got some watermelon in that hamper. I love watermelon!'

Meanwhile, Jonathan had met up with his friend, Andrew, and they were on the way into town. By way of making conversation, he asked, 'Got your harvest in yet?'

'Yes,' Andrew told him. And only just in the nick of time. My dad reckons the rains are coming early this year. What about you?'

'Just one corner of a field left,' answered Jonathan.

'Well, I hope you get it done in time,' Andrew told him. 'The weather's really closing in, now.'

'Oh, don't worry,' said Jonathan. 'Ben will do it.'

As they kept on walking, Jonathan kept thinking, 'I'm sure Ben will do it . . . I expect

Ben will do it . . . I hope Ben will do it.' Yet all the time, there was this nagging little voice saying, 'But what if he wants a day off, too?'

As they walked, Jonathan could feel the wind getting stronger; a sure indication that rain was very close. Gradually he realised that he wasn't going to enjoy his day out one little bit, because he'd be too worried about the farm.

'Sorry, Andy – gotta go!' he said, and turned on his heel without another word to run back to the farm.

Jonathan's father was very angry. He'd gone to the field to see how Ben was getting on, and take him a bit of lunch, and found nobody there. As the warm wind swirled around him, he knew there wasn't an hour to lose.

- He *rolled up his right sleeve*
- he *rolled up his left sleeve*
- and he started to *cut the corn with a sickle*

Before long, his back was aching and his right arm felt as if it were dropping off, but he dared not slow down. Eventually, he realised there was no way he would get all that corn harvested in time. 'If Ben had come here when he said he would,' he thought angrily, 'then it would be done by now.' Just then, he heard footsteps and turned to see Jonathan approaching with another sickle in his hand.

Father and son worked together against the strengthening wind, and the sun was just falling behind the mountain to the west as they stacked up the last of the corn and closed the barn door. Walking back to the house, they met Ben returning from his picnic. 'You look hot,' he said cheerily. 'Been working hard?'

His brother and father tried not to get angry, and explained what they had been doing.

'You didn't need to do that,' he said airily. 'I'd have done it sometime.'

As he said it, the first large, heavy drops of warm rain started to fall on them. '*Sometime* would have been too late,' grumbled Dad.

Ben was embarrassed, and tried to cover it up by getting angry. 'Don't blame me!' he said. 'At least I was willing, and didn't just say no, like someone else I could mention.'

'Ah,' said Dad, 'but in the end what you *say* isn't what matters – it's what you *do*.'

Our Story

Draw attention to the display, and let the children have a good laugh at the excuses. That's what they sometimes sound like although they probably don't realise it at the time! Sometimes, rather than spend time and effort on trying to avoid work, we'd be better off just getting on with it!

Prayers

Let's Chat

Most of us mean well.
We like to help,
and we really mean it when we say 'Yes'.
But is it really helpful
if we say 'yes' too easily,
and then don't actually do it?

We're Glad

Thank you, God, for keeping your promises.
You say you will always love us,
and you do.
Help us to be reliable, too,
so that other people know your love
and your faithfulness through us.

We're Sad

We all let people down sometimes.
That's not an excuse; just a fact.
Forgive us, if people have been hurt
because of our carelessness,
and help us to make amends
in the future.

Let's Pray for People

Loving God,
some people have to do jobs
that they really don't want to do at all.
Please help them to see
how important their work is,
and help us always to appreciate them.

Songs

Be the centre of my life
Do what you know is right
Let us talents and tongues employ
Seek ye first the kingdom of God

Will He or Won't He?

God's Story

Narrator	Jonathan was looking forward to a day off. He worked with his father and brother on the family farm, and they'd been really busy with the harvest. Now, they'd only got a corner of one field left to do and there was plenty of time before the rains came, so why shouldn't he have a day off? Then Dad called him.
Dad	Just one more big push today and we'll have it done. You get started in the field, and I'll stay here and get the barn ready, so we can get the corn stored properly.
Jonathan	Sorry, Dad, I'm going out.
Dad	If we don't get this last field done in time, we could be ruined! Ben, would you mind doing it?
Ben	Of course, Dad – no problem! Don't worry, I'm not selfish like Jonathan. You can rely on me.
Narrator	On the way to the farm, Ben met Rebecca, the daughter of the farmer next door.
Rebecca	Hi, Ben, fancy going for a picnic?
Ben	I'd love to, but I've got to go and work in the fields.
Rebecca	Oh, and it would have been so nice – just the two of us.
Ben	Why should I work, if Jonathan isn't! Come on, Rebecca; I hope you've got some watermelon in that hamper. I love watermelon!
Narrator	Meanwhile, Jonathan had met up with his friend, Andrew, and they were on the way into town.
Jonathan	Got your harvest in yet?
Andrew	Yes, and only just in time. My dad reckons the rains are coming early this year. What about you?
Jonathan	Just one corner of a field left.
Andrew	Well, I hope you get it done in time.
Jonathan	Oh, don't worry, Ben will do it.

Narrator	As they kept on walking, Jonathan kept hearing a nagging little voice saying, 'But what if he wants a day off, too?' He could feel the wind getting stronger; a sure indication that rain was very close. Gradually he realised that he wasn't going to enjoy his day out one little bit, because he'd be too worried about the farm.
Jonathan	Sorry, Andy – gotta go!
Narrator	Jonathan turned on his heel without another word and ran back to the farm. Meanwhile, Jonathan's father was very angry. He'd gone to the field to see how Ben was getting on, and take him a bit of lunch, and found nobody there. As the warm wind swirled around him, he knew there wasn't an hour to lose.

- He *rolled up his right sleeve*
- he *rolled up his left sleeve*
- and he started to *cut the corn with a sickle*

Before long, his back was aching and his right arm felt as if it were dropping off, but he dared not slow down. Eventually, he realised there was no way he would get all that corn harvested in time.

Dad	If Ben had come here when he said he would, then it would be done by now.
Narrator	Just then, he heard footsteps and turned to see Jonathan approaching with another sickle in his hand. Father and son worked together against the strengthening wind, and the sun was just falling behind the mountain to the west as they stacked up the last of the corn and closed the barn door. Walking back to the house, they met Ben returning from his picnic.
Ben	You look hot. Been working hard? You didn't need to do that – I'd have done it sometime. Oh, is that rain?
Dad	*Sometime* would have been too late.
Ben	Don't blame me! At least I was willing, and didn't just say no, like someone else I could mention.
Dad	Ah, but in the end what you *say* isn't what matters – it's what you *do*.

Speechless, but Not Dumb!

Based on Mark 7:31-37

BEFORE THE DAY

Try to collect information from organisations for disabled people. Study it with the children and write or draw their reactions to it. Display some of the information and the reactions at the assembly.

• Think about the actions for all the children to join in during the story.

ON THE DAY

Introduction

We're going to think about disability today. First, we'll say our 'Thank you' Prayer.

'Thank you' Prayer

Thank you, God, for all you give us,
thank you for the earth and sea;
thank you, God, for special people,
thank you, God, for making me.

God's Story

Thaddeus was fed up with being talked about as if he weren't there. Although he was deaf, Thaddeus always knew when that was happening by the way people glanced at him and the looks on their faces. Because he was deaf, he'd learnt to use his eyes better than most people, and he was always very clued up about what was going on. The trouble was that, because he couldn't hear, he'd never been able to speak, either. And because of that, he had never been able to have a job. Everyone just thought that because he couldn't hear or talk he must be completely stupid and useless. And that was really silly, because:

• His hands were fine *(click fingers)*
• he could see perfectly well *(point to eyes)*
• and he had a *really good brain (point to head)*

So Thaddeus had to beg for a living, and that was really hard. His friend Sue had made him a sign to show to people saying that he couldn't speak or hear and asking if they could spare any cash. Some people were nice about it and gave him a bit of money; others would occasionally buy him some food, or get his clothes washed for him. Other people, though, would brush him aside. Some would call him names, thinking he couldn't understand: names like 'layabout' and 'scrounger'. A lot of people didn't even think he really was disabled, and they would do and say horrible things to try and make him talk. Altogether, it was a terrible life.

Sue and her husband Dan were really worried about Thaddeus, and did all they could to help him, but they knew it wasn't enough.

'Perhaps we could do a sponsored camel ride to buy him some new clothes?' suggested Dan.

'Been there, done that,' replied Sue, gloomily. 'Anyway, how d'you think Thaddeus feels, being a charity case all the time?'

'I agree,' said Dan. 'I wish I'd got half the brain he has, but he just never gets the chance to use it.'

'What we really need,' said Sue, 'is a miracle.'

'In that case, you want Jesus,' came a voice from behind them.

Sue turned round and saw a stranger standing there. 'How long have you been eavesdropping?' she asked.

'Couldn't help overhearing,' came the reply. 'Now, you can make of this what you will, but I've got a friend who can cure things like deafness.'

'You wouldn't be winding us up, by any chance?' Dan queried.

'I don't wind people up,' the stranger answered. 'They work better if you don't. Look, d'you want to know more or not?'

'I'm not sure,' Sue mused. 'If we raise Thaddeus's hopes and then nothing happens . . .'

'He'd be even worse off than before,' concluded Dan. 'I'm not sure it's a good idea.'

It was happening again! Thaddeus was standing right there, and even his best friends were talking about him as if he were their pet poodle!

'Well, it's up to you,' said the stranger, 'but just don't say I never gave you the chance. Jesus is in town at the moment, but he won't be by tomorrow. So make your mind up.'

The stranger turned to walk off, stopped and came back. 'I should warn you, though,' he said, 'that if you meet Jesus your life won't be the same again. I was a fisherman on lake Galilee, working with my brother Simon, before Jesus came along. Now, I never know from one day to the next where I'm going to be or what I'm going to be doing.'

'Well, Thaddeus *always* knows that,' thought Sue, 'and a lot of good it does him!'

So it was that they brought Thaddeus to Jesus.

Jesus took Thaddeus's hand, and said, 'It must be like being in prison – I bet you hate it, don't you?'

Thaddeus couldn't understand what Jesus was saying, but he knew that he was being talked *to*, and not about. And that was enough to make him think that Jesus might be worth knowing better, so he smiled and nodded in appreciation.

Of course, Jesus was famous as a healer, and most people knew Thaddeus; so a crowd started to gather immediately.

'This won't do,' said Jesus. 'Miracles are my business, not circus stunts! Andrew, you and Simon keep these folk occupied while we find somewhere private.'

There was an alleyway nearby where Simon and Andrew could easily keep the crowd back, and Jesus took Thaddeus there. First, he put his fingers into Thaddeus's ears. Next, he licked his finger and placed it on Thaddeus's tongue; not exactly clinically hygienic, perhaps, but Thaddeus didn't mind. At least he was being taken seriously for a change!

'Yes,' Jesus murmured, 'just like a prison. Well, there's only one thing to do with prisons.' Then his voice became stronger as though he was giving an order. 'Be opened.'

Suddenly, Thaddeus had a completely new experience. His head was filled with a jumble of sounds: people's voices, babies crying, dogs barking, hooves and wheels clattering past in the square. His eyes lit up, and he said, 'Is that the "music" Sue and Dan have told me about?' Then he looked completely shocked. 'I can talk!'

Jesus smiled, and took Thaddeus back to his friends. People were amazed and delighted, and couldn't stop saying what a wonderful thing had happened. And the best part of all for Thaddeus was that they were saying it *to* him. He wouldn't need to be left out of things any more!

Our Story

Talk about the display material and the children's reactions to it. Are there things we can learn about the way we treat people who have disabilities?

Prayers

We're Glad

Thank you, God, for sending Jesus
to show us how much you love *all* people.
Help us to be like him,
and to value everyone we meet
as a human being.

We're Sad

Please forgive us, God,
if we've ever treated people badly
just because they're disabled.
Help us not to take our own fitness
and our abilities for granted,
and teach us to look out for positive qualities
in the people we meet.

Let's Pray for People

We pray for people who are disabled
by other people's attitudes
more than their own difficulties.
Please, God, give them strength
and confidence in themselves
and in you.

Songs

Brother, sister, let me serve you
Father, I place into your hands
Jesus had all kinds of friends
When I needed a neighbour

Speechless, but Not Dumb!

God's Story

Narrator   Thaddeus was fed up with being talked about as if he weren't there. Everyone thought that just because he couldn't hear or talk he must be completely stupid and useless. And that was really silly, because:

- His hands were fine *(click fingers)*
- he could see perfectly well *(point to eyes)*
- and he had a *really good brain (point to head)*

So Thaddeus had to beg for a living, and that was really hard. Some people called him names like 'layabout' and 'scrounger', thinking he couldn't understand. His friend Sue and her husband Dan did all they could to help him.

Dan   Perhaps we could do a sponsored camel ride for him?

Sue   Been there, done that. Anyway, how d'you think Thaddeus feels, being a charity case all the time?

Dan   I agree. I wish I'd got half the brain he has!

Sue   What we really need is a miracle.

Andrew   In that case, you want Jesus.

Sue   How long have you been eavesdropping?

Andrew   Couldn't help overhearing. Andrew's the name. Now, I've got a friend who can cure things like deafness.

Dan   You wouldn't be winding us up, by any chance?

Andrew   I don't wind people up – they work better if you don't. Look, d'you want to know more or not?

Sue   I'm not sure. If we raise Thaddeus's hopes and then nothing happens . . .

Dan   He'd be even worse off than before. I'm not sure it's a good idea.

Narrator   It was happening again! Thaddeus was standing right there, and even his best friends were talking about him as if he were their pet poodle!

Andrew   Well, it's up to you. I should warn you, though, that if you meet Jesus your life won't be the same again. I was a fisherman on Lake Galilee, with my brother Simon, before I met Jesus. Now, I never know from one day to the next where I'm going to be or what I'm going to do.

Sue   Thaddeus *always* does, and a lot of good it does him!

Narrator   So it was that they brought Thaddeus to Jesus.

Jesus   It must be like being in prison – I bet you hate it.

Narrator   Thaddeus couldn't understand what Jesus was saying, but he knew that he was being talked *to*, and not about. And that made him think that Jesus might be worth knowing better, so he smiled and nodded. Of course, Jesus was famous as a healer, and most people knew Thaddeus; so a crowd started to gather immediately.

Jesus   This won't do! Miracles are my business, not circus stunts! Let's find somewhere private.

Narrator   There was an alleyway nearby where Simon and Andrew could easily keep the crowd back, and Jesus took Thaddeus there. First, he put his fingers into Thaddeus's ears. Next, he licked his finger and placed it on Thaddeus's tongue; not exactly clinically hygienic, perhaps, but Thaddeus didn't mind. At least he was being taken seriously for a change!

Jesus   *(Thoughtfully)* Yes, just like a prison. Well, there's only one thing to do with prisons. *(Loudly and firmly)* Be opened.

Narrator   Suddenly, Thaddeus had a completely new experience. His head was filled with a jumble of sounds: people's voices, babies crying, dogs barking, hooves and wheels clattering past in the square.

Thaddeus   Is that the 'music' Sue and Dan have told me about? Hey! I can talk!

Narrator   People were amazed and delighted, and couldn't stop talking about what had happened. And the best part of all for Thaddeus was that they were saying it *to* him. He wouldn't need to be left out of things any more!

A Mite More Generous

Based on Mark 12:41-44

BEFORE THE DAY

Do the children know stories of acts of kindness? Perhaps they've experienced something, or read about it? The local 'freebie' press is often a good source of such stories. Look for 'little' things done by 'ordinary' people, and get them to write or draw their stories, which you can make into a display.

• Think about the actions for all the children to join in during the story.

ON THE DAY

Introduction

We're going to think about generosity today. First, we'll say our 'Thank you' Prayer.

'Thank you' Prayer

Thank you, God, for all you give us,
thank you for the earth and sea;
thank you, God, for special people,
thank you, God, for making me.

God's Story

There was great excitement in the town of Barton under Marsh. The famous television personality Ronnie Squareface was coming to present a very special award. And the best part of it all was that no one knew who had won it.

It had all begun when the Prime Minister had decided to give a special honour to the most generous person in the country. Lots of people wanted to win it. Wouldn't it be nice to be called the Most Generous Person? They could have headed notepaper printed, with 'MGP' after their name, and would probably be invited onto television chat shows so that they could talk about how generous they were.

There were a number of likely winners. The rock star Mickey Megabucks was known to have given away, ooh, at least fifty million pounds. Well, that was what the newspapers said, so it had to be true, didn't it? Then there was Doug Digwell, who'd made his fortune in swimming pools. He'd been splashing out millions as well. And Les Cargo, the edible snail merchant (it was the snails that were edible, not Les) was said to have shelled out a fortune.

The real favourite was Ivor Bank, chief executive of the recently privatised national mint. The word was that he'd given away his entire pay rise – and that came to a great deal more than all the others put together. He'd worked very hard at it, as well, making sure that good stories about him kept appearing in the news. He always pretended to be surprised of course. 'What?' he would say, smiling in a shy sort of way. 'How did you ever come to hear about that?' Altogether, Ivor knew he'd done very well and he was quite sure he'd win the title of 'Most Generous Person'.

Imagine the excitement when it was announced that the winner would be named at the presentation ceremony, which was to take place at Barton under Marsh. Now that was surprising. None of the famously generous people lived in Barton. Still it was probably because of the facilities: lots of open space and plenty of bed and breakfast places. Yes, that must be why it had been chosen. The day of the presentation was declared a public holiday so that everybody who wanted to could go.

In the audience at the presentation was Alice Fairbrother. She wanted to see who had won, because she liked generous people. She often used to wish she had more money, just so that she could give it away, but since her husband had been killed in an accident she had been too busy trying to look after the family to spend time making money, even for that purpose. She gave what she could to her church, and always managed to find a pound or two to give to the charity collectors who called, but felt sad that she couldn't do more than she did. Still, she would enjoy celebrating other people's generosity at the ceremony.

Before the presentation, there was lots of entertainment: singers, magicians, comedians and even some Members of Parliament who had always really wanted to be in show business, all took part in the festival. Everyone wanted to be seen in the same place as the Most Generous Person – whoever it turned out to be. Then the moment came. There was a big roll on the drums, a fanfare of trumpets and Ronnie Squareface stepped forward to open the envelope. Everyone held their breath. Mickey Megabucks was ready to sing a special celebration song when he won; Doug Digwell was trying to imagine the big swimming pool they would build to honour his achievement; Les Cargo was running through the menu for the banquet to celebrate his award; and Ivor Bank was so confident that he was out of his seat and on his way to the front before the announcement was even made.

'And the Most Generous Person award goes to . . .' Ronnie Squareface hesitated for a moment, 'Mrs Alice Fairbrother.'

'Ooh, I say,' thought Alice. 'Fancy there being someone else with the same name as me.' She looked around, but didn't see anyone going to the front, only Ivor Bank trying to sneak back to his seat without his embarrassment being noticed. As the applause died down, Squareface tried again. 'Mrs Alice Fairbrother.' More applause, and still nobody went forward. Then one of the officials came rushing up to Alice. 'Go on,' he hissed. 'What are you waiting for?'

Alice still thought it was someone else.

- She *looked to her left*
- she *looked to her right*
- then she *pointed to herself*

'Who, me? It can't be me.' But it was. When they finally got her to the front, Ronnie Squareface read out what was on the card. 'Mrs Alice Fairbrother is this year's Most Generous Person, because she has given as much as she can possibly afford.'

You can imagine how the others felt! Mickey Megabucks retired to his private island and refused to sing ever again. Doug Digwell sacked his team of lawyers; Les Cargo cut the salaries of all his accountants, and Ivor Bank said he was going to put up his interest rates until he'd got all his money back – and

that might take at least a couple of days.

As for Alice: well, she just couldn't work out what all the fuss was about.

Our Story

Point out the display, and emphasise that these are all stories about 'ordinary' people doing 'little' things for others. None of them is ever likely to get a reward, but then that's not why they did those things.

Prayers

We're Glad

Thank you, God,
for loving us so much
and being happy with
whatever we can give,
great or small.

We're Sad

We're sorry, God,
for sometimes thinking
that things like wealth and fame
are the most important.
Help us to value people for themselves.

Let's Pray for People

Loving God,
we pray for people who are unhappy
because they think the little they can give
isn't enough to make a difference.
Help them to know
how much you love them
and value their gifts.

Songs

Brother, sister, let me serve you
I come like a beggar
We're going to shine like the sun
When I needed a neighbour

A Mite More Generous

God's Story

Narrator	There was great excitement in the town of Barton under Marsh. The famous television personality Ronnie Squareface was coming to present a special award. And the best part of all was that no one knew who had won it.
Ronnie	Well, folks, here we are at Barton under Marsh for the first ever Most Generous Person award. The name of the mystery winner will be revealed soon, but I have here some of the favourites for the honour. First, the well-known rock star, Mickey Megabucks. Hello, Mickey. According to the papers you've given away, ooh, at least fifty million pounds. Is that true?
Mickey	Well, it's in the papers, innit?
Ronnie	Quite. And also here is Doug Digwell, who made his fortune in swimming pools. Hello, Doug.
Doug	Hi, Ron. Yes, I've been splashing out millions as usual for wonderful, deserving poor people.
Ronnie	Yes. And next, Les Cargo, the edible snail merchant (it's the snails that are edible, not Les).
Les	I've shelled out a fortune, but I don't like to talk about it.
Ronnie	But the real favourite is Ivor Bank, chief executive of the recently privatised national mint. The word is that he's given away a great deal more than all the others put together – he's given his entire pay rise for this year.
Ivor	*(With false modesty)* How did you ever hear about that?
Ronnie	From the person you paid to leak it to the press. Anyway, here we are at Barton under Marsh. Now that seems surprising since none of the favourites live here, but it does have lots of open space and plenty of hotels. And now we're ready to begin the presentation.
Narrator	In the audience was Alice Fairbrother. She wanted to see who had won, because she liked generous people.

Alice	Oh, I wish I had money to give away like that.
Narrator	Since her husband had been killed in an accident she had been too busy trying to look after the family to spend time making money, even for that purpose. She gave what she could to her church, and always managed to find a pound or two to give to the charity collectors who called, but felt sad that she couldn't do more.
Alice	I'll enjoy celebrating other people's generosity today.
Narrator	There was a big roll on the drums, a fanfare of trumpets and Ronnie Squareface stepped forward to open the envelope.
Ronnie	Well, folks, the Most Generous Person award goes to . . . Mrs Alice Fairbrother.
Alice	Ooh, I say! Fancy there being someone else with the same name as me.
Ronnie	Mrs Alice Fairbrother.
Narrator	Alice looked around, but didn't see anyone going forward. Then one of the officials came rushing up
Steward	Go on. What are you waiting for?
Narrator	Alice still thought it was someone else.

- She *looked to her left*
- she *looked to her right*
- then she *pointed to herself*

Alice	Who, me?
Ronnie	Mrs Alice Fairbrother is this year's Most Generous Person, because she has given as much as she can possibly afford.
Narrator	You can imagine how the others felt! Mickey Megabucks retired to his private island and refused to sing ever again. Doug Digwell sacked his team of lawyers; Les Cargo cut the salaries of all his accountants, and Ivor Bank said he was going to put up his interest rates until he'd got all his money back – and that might take at least a couple of days. As for Alice: well, she just couldn't work out what all the fuss was about.

Cherubs at Christmas

Based on the Matthew and Luke birth narratives

BEFORE THE DAY

Think about the kind of 'saviours' children know of: Superman, Batman, Wonderwoman, etc. There are various possibilities for this. You could use the children's own toys, if you are confident none will go astray. Alternatively you could get the children to draw their 'saviour' figures or, if you want to be really ambitious they could dress up as them. One way or another, have the examples ready for the assembly, and have a traditional Christmas image available for contrast.

- Think about the actions for all the children to join in during the story.

ON THE DAY

Introduction

Look at all these people who've tried to save the world. We're going to hear about God's saviour soon, but first, we'll say our 'Thank you' Prayer.

'Thank you' Prayer

Thank you, God, for all you give us,
thank you for the earth and sea;
thank you, God, for special people,
thank you, God, for making me.

God's Story

Hello, I'm Charlie and I'm a cherub. Yes, I know, your mum *might* have said that about you, but I'm a real one: halo, wings, chubby cheeks, the works. Honest! And I want to tell you about this amazing adventure I had.

Now, I'd known for quite a while that God was going to do something special. The world was in a pretty sorry state, and seemed to be going from bad to worse. Actually it wasn't – it's never been that simple – but it seemed like it at times. But when you've known God as long as I have you realise that he doesn't just let things get out of hand. I knew that he'd do something at the right time.

When he said the time had come, we all started hoping we'd get a good part to play. You never saw anything like it.

- We had to *wash our faces*
- we had to *comb our hair*
- and we had to *straighten our haloes*

My friend Gloria spent so much time in the shower that her wing feathers started to split at the ends. Mind you, we all knew who'd get the *really* plum job. It had to be Gabriel. He's very experienced – been around for a long time. *He's ever so old!* Don't say I said that, though, will you? Anyway, Gabriel was sent to earth with a message for a girl called Mary. You've never seen so many angels eavesdropping before – we all wanted to know what was going to happen!

Well, we could hardly believe what we overheard! With all the trouble the world was in, God was sending a *baby* of all things! Still, as time went on, we all began to get excited again. After all, everyone loves a baby – and this was a very special one! One thing puzzled us, though. We'd somehow got the idea that God's special man was going to come from Bethlehem – where David had come from. But Gabriel had gone to a couple in Nazareth – a carpenter called Joseph and his wife Mary. Still, we might have known that God had got that covered as well. Joseph, it turned out, had actually been born in Bethlehem, and he was going to have to go back there at just the time the baby was due. The government was going to count all the people, and that meant they had to return to where they had been born – rather like in school when you go to your classroom for registration. Now at first that seemed like a very neat solution to the problem, even though the last-minute timing didn't exactly allow for unexpected delays – but nearer the time I began to get anxious again. The census meant that half the world seemed to be going to Bethlehem, and there was nowhere to stay! Some of the younger cherubs were so sure God had got it wrong that I actually had a word with Gabriel. He reminded me that God always likes to be with the worst-off people, so ending up homeless, instead of in a nice warm hotel with room service and *en suite* was just what we should have expected. And that's how it turned out. The baby Jesus was born in a stable and they had to use a feeding trough for a cradle. I'm not sure who I felt most sorry for: Jesus having to lie in hay that the animals had been chewing, or for the animals themselves. I suppose for them having a baby in their dinner is a bit like people having a fly in their soup.

I was just thinking our job was over when Gabriel said, 'Not so fast – I've got work for you to do – go and get together five divisions of angels, and meet me on Cloud Seven in half an hour. Oh, and do try to choose some that have got half-decent singing voices.' As it happened, most of the angels were actually on Cloud Nine, and I had quite a job getting them to come down a peg or two, but they eventually did. Then Gabriel put me in charge, and told me to go and announce to the world what was happening. Well, we were halfway to the big church in Jerusalem when Gabriel came chasing after us – he caught us, too, which was no small achievement at his age. Apparently, we'd got it wrong. He told us it was time we understood that God works with the least important people – not the big-wigs. So we got redirected to a field with some shepherds in it. I suppose God knows best, but I wouldn't have wanted them around if *I* were having a baby – nasty smelly people, they were. Still, we did as we were told.

Well, after that, I spent a bit of time on sentry duty at the stable. Joseph and Mary didn't know I was there, of course, and I got a ringside seat. A lot of the time, it was quite boring really. Babies tend to sleep a lot, and – don't tell a soul I said this will you? – they all tend to look very much the same to me, even if they are as special as this one. But while I was there – just as I was thinking I might be better off doing something else – in came these amazing people. I thought I'd seen most things, but I'd never seen anything like this. They weren't from Israel – foreign people, I think, and pagan at that. It turned out they read the stars. I didn't think God approved of that sort of thing, but you live and learn, don't you? Anyway, when they came in, they told us about their journey – and about how they'd stopped at King Herod's palace to ask directions and he'd been really interested

and wanted to come and worship Jesus himself.

When I heard that, I pricked my ears up. Bad news, that Herod fellow – insanely jealous of anyone who may seem more important than he is. I didn't believe for a moment that he really wanted to come and worship Jesus. So when the wise men were sleeping, I had a word in the ear of one of them. 'Don't trust him,' I said. 'Not a nice man,' I said. 'Doesn't play by the rules,' I said. 'Take my advice,' I said, 'go home the pretty way.' So that's what they did, and I got a pat on the back from Gabriel for using my initiative, which is quite a rare event – a pat on the back from Gabriel, that is, not my using my initiative. I think God was pleased with me, too.

Our Story

Point out the display again, and then remind the children that God's way was different: no heroics, no power games, just love. And the people he used were a lot more ordinary than any of those!

Prayers

We're Glad

Thank you, God, for showing us
that no one's unimportant,
and no one should be left out.
Thank you for using ordinary people
and simple places.

We're Sad

Sometimes, Jesus, we get big ideas:
simple things aren't good enough for us.
But a stable was a good enough home for you,
and a feeding trough was a good enough cradle.
Forgive us for being too difficult to please.

Let's Pray for People

Please God, bless all homeless people.
Remind us, when we see them,
that we are seeing you, too.

Songs

Born in the night
Everyone's a Christmas Baby
Joy to the world
The angel Gabriel from heaven came

Cherubs at Christmas

God's Story

Charlie	Hello, I'm Charlie and this is Gloria, and we're angels.
Gloria	We want to tell you about our amazing adventure.
Charlie	We'd always known God was going to do something. The world seemed to be going from bad to worse.
Gloria	But we knew he'd do something at the right time.
Charlie	When he said the time had come, we all hoped we'd get a good part to play. You never saw anything like it.

- We had to *wash our faces*
- we had to *comb our hair*
- and we had to *straighten our haloes*

Charlie	Gloria spent so much time in the shower that her wing feathers started to split at the ends.
Gloria	Ooh, you little liar. I didn't!
Charlie	Oh yes, you did!
Gloria	Well, Gabriel would get the *really* plum job. He's very experienced – been around for a long time.
Charlie	*He's ever so old!* Don't say I said that, though, will you?*
Gloria	*I* will!
Charlie	Don't you dare!
Gloria	Anyway, Gabriel took a message to a girl called Mary, in Nazareth. Unbelievable! With all the trouble the world was in, God was sending a *baby* of all things!
Charlie	Now, we'd thought that Jesus was going to come from Bethlehem, not Nazareth. But as it turned out, Mary and Joseph were going to have to go there at just the time the baby was due – something about registrations, I think.
Gloria	Trouble was, Bethlehem was full and there was nowhere to stay. But Gabriel assured us God hadn't got it wrong.

* Encourage the children to promise to keep the secret.

Gabriel	God always likes to be with the worst-off people, so ending up homeless is just what you should expect.
Gloria	And that's how it turned out. The baby Jesus was born in a stable and they had to use a feeding trough for a cradle.
Charlie	I felt sorry for the animals. I suppose having a baby in their dinner is a bit like people having a fly in their soup. Before I could say so, Gabriel had a job for us.
Gabriel	Go and get five divisions of angels – preferably decent singers – and meet me on Cloud Seven in half an hour.
Charlie	Actually, most of the angels were on Cloud Nine, but we managed to get them down a peg or two.
Gabriel	Now go and announce to the world what's happening.
Charlie	Well, we were halfway to the big church in Jerusalem when Gabriel came chasing after us – he caught us, too, which was no small achievement at his age.
Gabriel	You've got it wrong. Worst-off people – remember?
Gloria	So we got redirected to a field with some shepherds in it. I wouldn't have wanted them around if *I* were having a baby – nasty smelly people, they were.
Charlie	After that, we spent a bit of time on sentry duty at the stable. The next lot of visitors were foreign astrologers.
Gloria	I didn't think God approved of that, but you live and learn. They told us they'd asked directions at Herod's palace and he'd wanted to worship Jesus himself.
Charlie	Bad news, that Herod fellow – insanely jealous of anyone who may seem more important than he is. We didn't believe for a moment that he really wanted to come and worship Jesus. So when the wise men were sleeping, we had a word in their ears.
Gloria	Don't trust him. Take our advice – go home the pretty way. So they did, and we got a pat on the back from Gabriel for using our initiative, which is quite rare.
Charlie	A pat on the back from Gabriel, that is, not our using our initiative. I think God was pleased with us, too.

There's a Baby in My Dinner

Based on Luke 2:1-20

BEFORE THE DAY

Have any of the children recently acquired a new baby brother or sister? Discuss with them the pros and cons of having a baby arrive in the house. List them in two columns on a large sheet of paper.

• Think about the actions for all the children to join in during the story.

ON THE DAY

Introduction

We've got a story to tell you about a baby who got in the way – and still does. First, we'll say our 'Thank you' Prayer.

'Thank you' Prayer

Thank you, God, for all you give us,
thank you for the earth and sea;
thank you, God, for special people,
thank you, God, for making me.

God's Story

Why are human beings so obsessed with numbers? They count everything! You wouldn't find self-respecting donkeys wasting all our time counting things. Life's too short for that. Humans, though, well they'll count anything. I know a person, not very far away, who has lots of bags full of little bits of gold. I can't see the fascination, personally – when you've seen one bit of gold you've seen them all. But he spends hours every night counting them.

Now let me see, what was I working up to? Oh, yes – the census. That's how we came to be in the silly situation I'm in now. Apparently, the government had the bright idea of counting all the people. I mean, can you imagine it? How can you count people when they won't stand still for ten minutes at a time? Well, they decided to tell all the people to go back to the town where they were born and register their names, and my master, Joseph, comes from Bethlehem. Now, make no mistake, Bethlehem is a wonderful place to come from – a lousy place to go to, but wonderful to come from. Trouble was, we had to go to it. And now we're here.

To make matters worse, Joseph's wife Mary was nine months pregnant, and seemed to think that gave her the right to ride on my back everywhere. Now that's all very well, but when did you last see a pregnant donkey being given a piggyback by a human? Never. Precisely. It's species discrimination and I intend to make a complaint about it.

Anyway, that's how we came to be here. We had a terrible journey – not a service area in sight the whole way, and the road's been neglected for years. My feet are killing me – and I've got twice as many as you have! Still, we eventually got here, and I was really looking forward to a warm stable, some soft straw and a good square meal. Well, you'll never guess. All the rooms in the hotels were full – I told Joseph he should have booked, but would he listen? The first I knew about the problem was when I was just about to lie down on the straw and in came the innkeeper and offered Joseph and Mary my room. I don't know what the world's coming to. Not only that, but when the baby was born they put it to bed in my dinner! No kidding! Slapped it straight into the manger without so much as a 'by your leave'! Human beings really are an undeveloped species you know. I mean, we donkeys think nothing of having babies. We just get on with it, without fuss and bother, and when it's born it has to stand on its own feet – literally – straight away. These humans, though, you never saw such a carry-on. Still, I must admit there's something very special about a human baby – they're sweet little things. So naturally I wanted to have a look. I wandered over to the manger – it was meant to be for me, after all – and had a look inside. As I looked in I caught the smell of the hay, and thought I'd just get a quick nibble while I was there. You'd have thought I was doing something dreadful! Mary screamed, and

Joseph got hold of my collar and started to drag me away. I tell you I'd just about had enough. What with the walk, the invasion of my privacy and now I wasn't even allowed to eat a bit of my own food. So maybe I overreacted, I don't know, but I did something that comes very naturally to us donkeys. I dug my hooves into the earth floor and refused to move an inch. Even though my feet were hurting, it was worth it.

- Poor Joseph *pulled*
- and he *pulled*
- and he *pulled*!

I didn't know Joseph even knew some of the words he used! Very soon, the innkeeper and his wife came over to see what the fuss was about and I had a real live audience to play to, but they didn't stay long. The wife disappeared to the house and came back with a bucket of the most delicious-smelling oats you ever saw in your life. 'Well,' I thought. 'Somebody cares about me.' Then she went and put it the other side of the stable. Of course, I knew what the game was, but I decided I'd made my point. After all, donkeys are stubborn but we're not stupid. So I walked over to the bucket and had a good feed and pretended not to notice Joseph tying me up.

Anyway, things have improved a bit now. We've got some visitors, and Mary's letting them hold the baby which gives me a chance for a good look. Mind you, I'm not too happy about the visitors – they've got a distinct smell of sheep about them, and little bits of wool all over their clothes. They *say* they're shepherds, and they're telling some incredible story about angels coming to them and saying that a baby had been born. They *say* that they were so excited they left their flocks in the fields and came rushing over to see the baby. They certainly look and smell like shepherds, but I know their game. I mean, what shepherd who's any good leaves the sheep in the field at night without protection? Even if they did, they wouldn't admit it to strangers.

No – I've got their number. Oh, I'll admit they're playing the part very well, right down to the grass stains on their clothes and the mud on their sandals, but I've got them rumbled. I know travelling salesmen when I see them. You mark my words, before those people leave, Mary and Joseph will have spent money they can't afford on pretty little bootees and silly cardigans with lambs all over them – now donkeys I could understand.

(Do you think the donkey's right about the visitors?)

Our Story

Look at the lists. Like all good things, babies can inconvenience us somewhat. God's like that, too. He comes to love us, but he changes things, and sometimes we find him quite difficult to live with. But he's worth making the effort for!

Prayers

We're Glad
Thank you, God,
for making life such an adventure.
Thank you for the unexpected times
when what seemed like terrible problems
turn out to be your opportunities.
Help us to be more open to you.

We're Sad
We'd like to say 'sorry'
for always wanting to be comfortable
when you are trying to disturb us!
Sometimes you ask us to do things
we would rather not do,
or not to do things which we like.

Let's Pray for People
Some people only ever see the hard side of life,
and don't notice the good things all around
    them.
That's very sad.
Please, God, help people who are unhappy
to find something to smile about,
something to give them hope.

Songs

God was born on earth
Hee haw!
See him lying on a bed of straw
We wish you a merry Christmas

There's a Baby in My Dinner!

God's Story

Narrator   Why are human beings so obsessed with numbers? They count everything! You wouldn't find self-respecting donkeys wasting all our time counting things. Life's too short for that. Anyway, the government had the bright idea of counting all the people. Joseph and Mary weren't pleased.

Joseph   We've been told we've got to go to Bethlehem.

Mary   Whatever for?

Joseph   To be counted. We've all got to go back to the town we first came from.

Mary   Oh, great! And me about to have a baby!

Narrator   I'm not surprised Mary wasn't thrilled. Bethlehem is a wonderful place to come from – but it's a lousy place to *go to*. And now we're here. Mary rode the whole way here on my back. Now that's all very well, but when did you last see a pregnant donkey being given a piggyback by a human? Never. Precisely. It's species discrimination and I intend to make a complaint. But it got worse. I was just settling down in my stable when Mary and Joseph came in with the innkeeper.

Innkeeper   I'm sorry, but this is simply all I have available.

Joseph   Well it's not good enough.

Mary   Oh, do lay off, Joseph. I'm too tired to argue. This will just have to do.

Narrator   I tell you, I didn't believe it! I told Joseph right from the start he should have booked, but would he listen? And it got worse. When the baby was born they put it to bed in my dinner! No kidding! Slapped it straight into the manger without so much as a 'by your leave'! Still, I must admit there's something very special about a human baby – they're sweet little things. Naturally, I wanted to have a look, so I wandered over to the manger.

Mary   AAAAH! Get that dreadful animal away!

Narrator	She didn't say that when she was using me as a four-wheel drive on the way here! Joseph got hold of my collar and started to drag me away. I tell you I'd just about had enough. Maybe I overreacted, I don't know, but I dug my hooves into the earth floor and refused to move an inch.

- Joseph *pulled*
- and he *pulled*
- and he *pulled*

	but I just stood there. Boy, was he mad! Very soon, the innkeeper came to see what the fuss was about.
Innkeeper	Leave this to me. If I put this bucket of oats over here . . .
Narrator	Of course, I knew what the game was, but I'd made my point. After all, donkeys are stubborn but we're not stupid. So I walked over to the bucket and pretended not to notice Joseph tying me up. Then, just as I thought we might all get some sleep we had visitors. I ask you – at that time of night!
Shepherd 1	We don't want to be a nuisance.
Narrator	That means they're going to be.
Shepherd 2	We're shepherds, and while we were minding the sheep an angel told us this was a special baby.
Narrator	Oh, that's a good one! I haven't heard that one before. I mean, what shepherd who's any good leaves the sheep in the field at night unprotected? Even if they did, they wouldn't admit it.
Joseph	Oh, please come in. How kind of you!
Narrator	Easily taken in – that's his trouble. But I've got them rumbled. I know salesmen when I see them. You mark my words, before those people leave, Mary and Joseph will have spent money they can't afford on pretty little bootees with lambs all over them – now donkeys I could understand.

(Do you think the donkey's right about the visitors?)

Lovely Sermon, Rabbi

Based on Luke 4:14-30

BEFORE THE DAY

Gather some information, and talk with the children, about people of faith who have made themselves unpopular. Obvious examples are Desmond Tutu, Martin Luther King, Oscar Romero, Alan Paton. Perhaps you can get some pictures of them.

• Think about the actions for all the children to join in during the story.

ON THE DAY

Introduction

Sometimes, loving people can be hard, and we have to be very brave. We'll think more about that in a moment. First, we'll say our 'Thank you' Prayer.

'Thank you' Prayer

Thank you, God, for all you give us,
thank you for the earth and sea;
thank you, God, for special people,
thank you, God, for making me.

God's Story

Jerry was preparing to lead worship at the Nazareth synagogue, on the Sabbath day. He always liked to get other people to join in as much as he could and on this particular morning was wondering who should do the readings. As he stood in the porch, welcoming the congregation, he saw a familiar face.

'Hello,' said Jerry, 'so good to see you again. Would you do a reading for me? It'll be nice for you to use that lovely lectern you made for us.'

'Yes, it would,' said Jesus. 'I'd be pleased to read.'

So the service started, and when the time came Jerry smiled at Jesus and sat down. Jesus walked to the front and opened the big Bible. 'Now, let's see,' he thought. 'Something from Isaiah, I think.' He found the passage and began to read.

'The spirit of God is upon me, because he has chosen me to bring good news to all the poor, to announce that prisoners will be released and the blind will be able to see; to liberate all who are suffering, and say that God's promised time has come.'

Now, that wouldn't have caused any problems because they knew it was just a Bible reading and most people didn't take those very seriously. And if Jesus had just sat down and kept quiet everything would have stayed nice and comfortable. But Jesus wasn't one to do that kind of thing: if something needed to be said, he said it. And as far as he was concerned the Bible *was* to be taken seriously. So he went on to say some words of his own.

'Today,' he said, 'these words have come true right here and now.'

'Ooh,' exclaimed Jed, the local butcher, 'hasn't he got a lovely way with words.'

'Certainly has,' said the Tom, the baker. 'You'd hardly think he was just a carpenter, would you?'

'No,' added Ruth, another shopkeeper. 'But it's true, though. I know his mother – lovely person.'

'Keep quiet, woman!' ordered Jed. 'Who told you you could speak in the synagogue? And when are you going to finish my candlesticks?'

'I know what you're all thinking,' Jesus went on. 'You're going to ask me to do some trick or other, because you've heard I work the odd miracle here and there. Well, to begin with I'm not a performing monkey; and for another thing, no prophet has ever been taken seriously in his home town.'

Jerry was starting to wish he'd never asked Jesus to read in the first place.

• He *tried to look casual*
   then he *stroked his beard*
• then he *raised his hand* to catch Jesus' eye

'Oh, I don't think that's really true . . .' he began, trying to smooth things over a bit.

'No?' Jesus challenged him. 'Don't you think there were plenty of widows needing help in

Israel during Elijah's time? But God had to send him across the border to a foreign country.'

'I've had enough of this!' shouted Tom. 'I come to synagogue to have a good sing, not listen to home truths.'

But Jesus wasn't going to be put off, now he was in his stride.

'And what about Naaman the Syrian,' he demanded, 'who came to Elisha to be healed? Weren't there any patients in Israel at the time? So why did God choose a foreigner?'

That did it! If there's one way to get a congregation wound up it's to tell us that God finds outsiders easier to work with than we are! And this congregation were no exception. Before long, the whole place was in uproar. Jerry decided there was nothing he could do since nobody ever really listened to him, anyway, and slipped quietly out of the side door.

Tom pointed an accusing finger at Jesus. 'Come on, let's get him!'

The whole crowd surged forward and grasped hold of Jesus. His mother Mary, and his brothers, tried to stop them but they never had a chance. Jesus was bundled to the synagogue entrance and out down the street. As Mary watched, her blood ran cold because she knew they were taking him to the cliff outside the town. Nothing, it seemed, could stop them, now. On and on they rushed, pushing Jesus ahead of them, shouting insults as they went, until they got to the top of the hill and started towards the cliff edge.

It was a funny thing, but the calmest person in the whole crowd was Jesus himself. Tom, who was holding one of his arms, couldn't understand it. More than that, he didn't really see much point in doing all this if Jesus wasn't even going to have the decency to be frightened. When they got to the edge, Tom shouted above the noise of the crowd, 'All right, then! You apologise. Let's hear you beg for mercy.'

The crowd went quiet, waiting for Jesus to start grovelling. Instead, Jesus turned and fixed them with a steely glare. 'Would that prove that I was wrong?' he asked. 'Your behaviour is making my point much better than any words of mine ever could. You've just shown that everything I said is true. Now I suggest that you start behaving like adults – or at least

like mature twelve-year-olds. When you want to discuss this sensibly, you know where to find me. Now, let me through.'

Amazingly, they all did just as he said – looking rather embarrassed as he passed them. One or two squeezed his arm as if in apology, but no one dared look him in the eyes.

'Whose daft idea was all this, anyway?' Jed demanded.

'Truth hurts, doesn't it?' said Ruth. 'And by the way, you'll get your candlesticks when you've paid for the last ones you had.'

Our Story

Introduce the characters in the pictures, and show that following Jesus today might not mean always being nice to everyone! We might have to be quite courageous at times.

Prayers

We're Glad

Thank you, God,
for people whom we can believe;
people who we know wouldn't lie to us,
even for 'good' reasons.
It's great to know we can trust them.

We're Sad

Maybe we don't try to throw people
over cliffs, Jesus!
But we can still be touchy,
especially about criticism
when deep down we know it's true.
Please forgive us,
and help us to appreciate honesty.

Let's Pray for People

Loving God, please bless all people
who have difficult messages to speak.
Help them to be brave and honest,
and help those who need to hear
to listen openly.

Songs

Jesus will never, ever
Make me a channel of your peace
One more step along the world I go
You are the King of glory

Lovely Sermon, Rabbi

God's Story

Narrator Jerry was preparing to lead worship at the Nazareth synagogue, on the Sabbath day. As he stood welcoming the congregation, he saw a familiar face.

Jerry Hello, Jesus. Would you do a reading for me? It'll be nice for you to use that lovely lectern you made for us.

Jesus Yes, it would. I'd be pleased to read.

Narrator So the service started, and when the time came, Jesus walked to the front and opened the big Bible.

Jesus Now, let's see. Something from Isaiah, I think. Here we are. 'The Spirit of God is upon me, because he has chosen me to bring good news to all the poor, to announce that prisoners will be released and the blind will be able to see; to liberate all who are suffering, and say that God's promised time has come.' Today, these words have come true right here and now.

Narrator Jed and Tom, the local butcher and baker, were impressed.

Jed Ooh, hasn't he got a lovely way with words, Tom!

Tom Certainly has. You'd hardly think he was just a carpenter.

Ruth No, but it's true. I know his mother – lovely person.

Jed Keep quiet, Ruth! Women don't speak in the synagogue. And when are you going to finish my candlesticks?

Jesus I know what you're all thinking. You're going to ask me to do some trick or other, because you've heard I work the odd miracle here and there. Well, to begin with I'm not a performing monkey; and for another thing, no prophet has ever been taken seriously in his home town.

Narrator Jerry was starting to wish he'd never asked Jesus to read.

- He *tried to look casual*
- then he *stroked his beard*
- then he *raised his hand* to catch Jesus' eye

Jerry	Oh, I don't think that's really true.
Jesus	No? Don't you think there were plenty of widows needing help in Israel during Elijah's time? But God had to send him across the border to a foreign country.
Tom	I've had enough of this! I come to synagogue to have a good sing, not listen to home truths.
Jesus	And what about Naaman the Syrian, who came to Elisha to be healed? Weren't there any patients in Israel at the time? So why did God choose a foreigner?
Narrator	That did it! Before long, the whole place was in uproar.
Tom	Come on, let's get him!
Narrator	The whole crowd surged forward and grasped hold of Jesus. He was bundled outside and down the street. On and on they rushed, pushing Jesus ahead of them, shouting insults as they went, until they got to the top of the hill and started towards the cliff edge. It was a funny thing, but the calmest person in the whole crowd was Jesus himself. Tom, who was holding one of his arms, couldn't understand it. More than that, he didn't really see much point in doing all this if Jesus wasn't even going to have the decency to be frightened.
Tom	All right, then, Jesus! Let's hear you beg for mercy.
Narrator	The crowd went quiet, waiting for Jesus to start grovelling. Instead, Jesus fixed them with a steely glare.
Jesus	Would that prove me wrong? You've just shown that everything I said is true. When you want to discuss this like adults – or at least like mature twelve-year-olds – you know where to find me. Now, let me through.
Narrator	Amazingly, they all did just as he said – looking rather embarrassed as he passed them. No one dared look him in the eyes.
Jed	Whose daft idea was all this, anyway?
Ruth	Truth hurts, doesn't it? And by the way, you'll get your candlesticks when you've paid for the last ones you had.

Jesus Does Things Differently

Based on Luke 22:7-27

BEFORE THE DAY

Collect some 'men's' tools: spanners, hammers, chisels, etc., and some 'women's' ones: rolling pins, feather dusters, and so on. If you think it's safer, get the children to draw or paint them. Then, before the assembly, set them out on separate tables with a blue cloth for the men and a pink cloth for the women.

• Think about the actions for all the children to join in during the story.

ON THE DAY

Introduction

We're going to look at some old-fashioned ideas in a few minutes. First, we'll say our 'Thank you' Prayer.

'Thank you' Prayer

Thank you, God, for all you give us,
thank you for the earth and sea;
thank you, God, for special people,
thank you, God, for making me.

God's Story

Jesus and his friends had a lot to do: it was the time of the great Jewish festival called 'Passover'.

'Where are we going to have the special meal, Jesus?' asked Andrew. 'We'll need to go and start getting ready soon.'

'That's true,' said Jesus. 'Go into the city and look out for a man carrying a jar of water; he'll show you where to go.'

'A *man* carrying water?' scoffed Peter. 'That's women's work. No self-respecting man would be seen in public carrying water!'

'Then there shouldn't be too many, and you'll be quite sure that it's the right one when you find him, won't you?' said Jesus. 'I keep telling you that things are going to be different in our society – and that means that you men are going to have to pull your weight, for a start.'

Andrew and Peter went into the town and, sure enough, they saw a man carrying a big water jug on his shoulder, and they followed him.

'Er, excuse me,' said Andrew, a little hesitantly. 'Can I ask you something?'

'Don't tell me,' answered the man. 'You want to know why my wife doesn't do this job. Well, I don't see why women should have all the hard work to do, do you?'

'But don't you feel a bit of a wimp?' asked Peter. 'You know – doing women's work?'

'Wimp?' laughed the man. 'Have you felt the weight of one of these things?' Peter and Andrew had to admit that they never had. They followed the man into his house and he showed them up to the top floor where Andrew and Peter got busy setting the room out.

• Andrew *polished the table*
• Peter *poured out some wine*
• and Andrew *cut up some bread*

In the early evening, the rest of the group arrived with Jesus leading them, and they sat down to enjoy the special meal. That was when Jesus said something that really puzzled them.

He took the loaf of bread, and gripped it firmly in his hands, holding it up where they could all see it. 'This is my body,' he said. Then, before anyone could ask what on earth he was talking about, he ripped the loaf of bread in half.

'My body', he said, 'torn apart for your sake. I want you to remember me by doing this.'

They were very puzzled. What did he mean? Why would they need to remember him? Was he going away? Before they could ask, the main course was being served. Very soon, they were all chattering away and not really thinking about what Jesus had said.

'You mark my words,' said James, through a mouthful of roast lamb, 'Any day now, Jesus is going to be the top man. And I'm going to be his chief helper.'

'Oh no, you're not!' objected his brother John. 'I'm going to be top dog around here – after Jesus of course.'

'You're both wrong,' Peter interrupted 'He told me I would be – remember?'

'You!' scoffed Andrew. 'You're all talk, you are. Why, you're supposed to be a fisherman and Jesus can catch more fish than you – and he's a carpenter.'

'Well, I don't know what you're all arguing about,' said Matthew, in a superior sort of way. 'Jesus will need somebody with an education – and that's got to be me.'

'That'd be funny if it weren't so silly,' Peter objected. 'Everyone knows you're a traitor and a con-man. D'you think Jesus would trust you?'

Jesus got fed up with all the wrangling. 'Look,' he said, 'in the ordinary world, the important people give orders and make other people work for them. That's not how it will be with you, though. The greatest among you is going to have to be the slave of the rest. That's how I operate.'

'Oh, well, that wimp who showed us the way will be all right then – won't he!' laughed Peter.

'"Showed you the way" is right,' said Jesus. 'And if you want to be a leader you're going to have to be like him.'

Then Jesus took a jug of wine and poured it out into a large cup. He called for silence, and said a prayer of thanks to God before he offered the cup to his friends. As he did so, he started talking strangely again.

'This is my blood,' he said, 'which is poured out for you. Do this to remember me.'

He passed the cup round for them to share. It seemed a little odd, drinking out of that cup after what Jesus had said, but they knew him well enough to know that there was some very deep meaning in his words. Peter had an uneasy feeling that something very special was happening, and he began to feel a strange mixture of excitement and fear.

As they went out from there, towards the Garden of Gethsemane, Andrew said to Peter, 'What's going on, d'you think?'

'I don't know,' answered Peter, 'but I've got a feeling it will make that man carrying water look rather ordinary.'

Our Story

Look at the two tables. Isn't it odd to have special colours for boys and girls? And to think that once, boys couldn't learn cookery at school and girls couldn't learn woodwork! (It's not really all that long since women won the right to vote – and how they had to fight for that as well.)

But where Jesus is in charge we don't think like that . . . do we?

Prayers

We're Glad

Thank you, God, for caring for us,
giving us our food,
helping us in our lives,
showing us that we're important to you.

We're Sad

Please forgive us, God,
for the silly ideas we have,
and the way we cause people to suffer for them.
Help us to treat people as people.

Let's Pray for People

We pray for people who feel
they aren't important
because they have to take orders,
not give them.
Help them to remember
that the whole world would be poorer
if they weren't in it.

Songs

I'm black, I'm white, I'm short, I'm tall
Jesus had all kinds of friends
There are hundreds of sparrows
When God made the garden of creation

Jesus Does Things Differently

God's Story

Narrator	Jesus and his friends had a lot to do: it was the time of the great Jewish festival called 'Passover'.
Andrew	Where d'you want us to prepare the special meal, Jesus?
Jesus	Good question, Andrew. Go into the city and look out for a man carrying a jar of water; follow him.
Peter	Carrying water's women's work. No self-respecting man would be seen in public carrying water!
Jesus	Then there shouldn't be too many, Peter, should there? I keep telling you that things are going to be different in our society – and that means that you men are going to have to pull your weight, for a start.
Narrator	Sure enough, Andrew and Peter saw a man carrying a big water jug on his shoulder, and they followed him.
Andrew	Er, excuse me, can I ask you something?
Man	You want to know why my wife doesn't do this. I don't see why women should do all the hard work, do you?
Peter	But don't you feel a bit of a wimp? You know – doing women's work?
Man	Wimp? Have you felt the weight of one of these things?
Narrator	Peter and Andrew followed the man to the top floor of his house. They got busy setting the room out.

- Andrew *polished the table*
- Peter *poured out some wine*
- and Andrew *cut up some bread*

Later, at the meal, Jesus said something really puzzling. He took the loaf of bread, and ripped it in half.

Jesus	This is my body. My body, torn apart for your sake. I want you to remember me by doing this.

Peter	What's he talking about, Andrew?
Andrew	I dunno. What d'you think, James?
James	All I know is that any day now, Jesus is going to be the top man. And I'm going be his chief helper.
Peter	Oh no, you're not! He told me *I* would be – remember?
Andrew	You! You're all talk, you are. Why, you're supposed to be a fisherman and Jesus can catch more fish than you – and he's a carpenter.
Jesus	Look, in the ordinary world, the important people give orders and make other people work for them. That's not how it will be with you, though. The greatest among you is going to have to be the slave of the rest. That's how I operate.
Peter	Oh, well, that wimp who showed us the way will be all right then – won't he!
Jesus	'Showed you the way' is right. And if you want to be a leader you're going to have to be like him.
Narrator	Then Jesus took a jug of wine and poured it out into a large cup. He called for silence, and said a prayer of thanks to God before he offered the cup to his friends. As he did so, he started talking strangely again.
Jesus	This is my blood, which is poured out for you. Do this to remember me.
Narrator	He passed the cup round for them to share. It seemed a little odd, drinking out of that cup after what Jesus had said, but they knew him well enough to know that there was some very deep meaning in his words. Peter had an uneasy feeling that something very special was happening, and he began to feel a strange mixture of excitement and fear. They went out from there towards the Garden of Gethsemane.
Andrew	What's going on, d'you think, Peter?
Peter	I don't know, Andrew, but I've got a feeling it will make that man carrying water look rather ordinary.

Pipped at the Sheep Gate

Based on John 5:1-9

BEFORE THE DAY

Collect some wildlife pictures and make a colourful display. Include both predators and others, and try to put them uncomfortably close together, so that a picture of a lion, for example, might be right next to a gazelle.

• Think about the actions for all the children to join in during the story.

ON THE DAY

Introduction

Sometimes, this world can be a bit like a jungle. Before we think about that, let's say our 'Thank you' Prayer.

'Thank you' Prayer

Thank you, God, for all you give us,
thank you for the earth and sea;
thank you, God, for special people,
thank you, God, for making me.

God's Story

Bart wasn't having much luck. All he wanted was a dip in the pool. Not much to ask, is it? Part of the trouble was that he had to get in at exactly the right moment. This was a special pool, in Jerusalem, at a place called the Sheep Gate, and it was said that an angel came along every so often and stirred up the water. The first person into the pool while that was happening got cured of whatever was wrong with them.

Now there were a lot of people who wanted to get into the pool. Some were blind, others couldn't walk, and a few, like Bart, were paralysed. Bart just about had enough strength in his arms to drag himself along, but he was very slow. And no matter how close to the pool he lay, someone always seemed to pip him to the post. 'If only I could get in,' he thought, 'then perhaps I could help a few of these other people afterwards.'

As he lay there, he saw the ripples begin to spread across the surface of the pool. Frantically, he grabbed at the edge and tried to pull himself forward, but it was no good. He knew he'd lost when he heard the voice behind him.

'I say, gangway there, if you don't mind. I've simply got to cure my sore thumb.'

Bart turned his head and saw a young man in a beautiful fine coat running towards the pool.

As he got to the edge the man tore off his coat and plunged in. 'Oh, what a relief!' Bart heard him say. 'That's been hurting for a good hour, now, and I couldn't take it any more.'

'A good hour!' thought Bart. 'I've been paralysed like this for thirty-eight years, but what do thirty-seven years, eleven months, fifty-one weeks, six days and twenty-three hours matter?'

'I say, old chap, I seem to have forgotten my towel.' The stranger grinned down at Bart. 'Could I borrow yours?'

It was no good complaining, so Bart just smiled politely as the other man dried himself off. The pool would be rippled again in a few hours.

Bart fell asleep after that, and awoke to find a woman standing beside him. She was dressed in the most amazing, expensive clothes, and Bart felt sure that she couldn't be about to get into the water. She saw Bart's eyes open and flashed him a big smile.

'Oh, my dear, it's so awful; I've got such a *terrible* headache, and it's playing havoc with my social life. I say, you don't mind if I go first, do you, darling?'

Bart was amazed! 'You're going in the pool in those lovely clothes,' he said. 'You surely don't intend to take them off.'

The woman smiled mischievously. 'You should be so lucky, you naughty boy!' she said. 'Oh, the clothes don't matter – I can buy some more tomorrow if they shrink. I buy new clothes every day anyway.'

Bart was going to ask her what on earth she did with so many clothes, but the ripples appeared on the water and the woman stepped daintily into the pool. Or at least she *tried* to do that, but it was deeper than she thought and she fell in right over her head.

When she came up again,

- she *shook her head*
- she *pushed her hair back*
- and she *wiped her eyes*

'Oh dear, silly me!' she said. 'Now I'll *have* to buy a new outfit, won't I?'

As she walked away, leaving a trail of drips behind her, Bart wondered whether he would ever get into the water.

A little later, Bart saw someone else approaching: a man with a few friends. 'Oh, that's that!' thought Bart. 'He's got his own heavies. I wonder what's wrong with him: a bunion, perhaps, or a receding hairline?'

When the water rippled, the man stood still. Bart got angry. 'Look' he said, 'you may as well get on with it. At this rate neither of us is going to benefit.'

'Are you waiting to get in the pool?' asked the man.

'Well, actually I'm frying some chips,' said Bart, 'but come to think of it . . .'

He turned to give the man an angry stare, and found a pair of really kind eyes looking back at him.

'I'm sorry,' Bart mumbled, 'but I'm getting really fed up. I've been lying here for ages, and every time the water ripples someone else gets there first.'

'I'm not rushing to jump in,' observed the other man.

'Well, in that case could you help me?' Bart asked, hoping that he might yet be in time.

'Well, I suppose I could,' drawled the other, slowly. Bart was getting really angry now because the ripples were subsiding again. The man continued. 'Why don't you just get up and pick up that bed of yours and go home?'

That did it! Bart was furious! 'I'm going to give that man a piece of my mind!' he thought.

Before he knew what he was doing, Bart was on his feet and wagging an accusing finger in the man's face. The man didn't seem perturbed; in fact he appeared to be enjoying the whole thing. Then Bart realised that the smile playing around the stranger's lips was a genuine one, not a mocking one. 'There,' said the man. 'That wasn't so difficult, was it?'

The penny dropped. 'I'm standing up!' Bart thought. 'For the first time in thirty-eight years.'

He bent down to pick up his bed, and was half-way through rolling it up when he realised he hadn't thanked the stranger who had healed him. He straightened up again, and found himself standing alone. The mysterious healer had melted away into the crowd.

'Well,' thought Bart, 'fancy helping someone and not waiting around to take the credit. What a kind man!'

But then, as you and I know, that's the kind of person Jesus is.

Our Story

Point out the pictures. In the jungle, only the fittest survive: the best hunters, the fastest runners and so on. But if God had wanted us to live like that, he'd have put us in the jungle, wouldn't he?

Prayers

We're Glad

Thank you, God,
for people who care for others
for their sake,
and not for any glory or credit
they might gain through it.
Thank you for putting wonderful people
into the world.

We're Sad

We're all a little selfish occasionally,
and it's easy to take advantage
when you're relatively fit and healthy.
Please God, forgive us
when we make so much of our own troubles
and so little of other people's.

Let's Pray for People

We pray for people who are disadvantaged
by others whose fitness is greater
but whose needs are less.
Help us build a caring society.

Songs

Jesus put this song into our hearts
I, the Lord of sea and sky
There are people who live in mansions
When God made the garden of creation

Pipped at the Sheep Gate

God's Story

Narrator	Bart was beside a special pool, in Jerusalem, at a place called the Sheep Gate, and it was said that an angel came along every so often and stirred up the water. The first person into the pool while that was happening got cured of whatever was wrong with them. No matter how close to the edge he lay, someone always seemed to get in first. He saw the ripples begin to spread across the surface of the pool. Frantically, he grabbed at the edge and tried to pull himself forward, but it was no good.
Man	I say, gangway there, if you don't mind. I've simply got to cure my sore thumb.
Narrator	Bart turned his head and saw a young man in a beautiful fine coat running towards the pool. As he got to the edge the man tore off his coat and plunged in.
Man	Oh, what a relief! That's been hurting for a good hour, now, and I couldn't take it any more.
Bart	*(Aside)* A good hour! I've been like this for thirty-eight years, but what do thirty-seven years, eleven months, fifty-one weeks, six days and twenty-three hours matter?
Man	I say, old chap, could I borrow your towel?
Narrator	Bart fell asleep after that, and awoke to find a woman standing beside him. She flashed him a big smile.
Woman	Oh, my dear, it's so awful: I've got such a *terrible* headache, and it's playing havoc with my social life. I say, you don't mind if I go first, do you, darling?
Bart	You're going in the pool in those lovely clothes? And you surely don't intend to take them off?
Woman	You should be so lucky, you naughty boy! Oh, the clothes don't matter – I can buy some more tomorrow if they shrink. I buy new clothes every day anyway.
Narrator	When the ripples appeared on the water, the woman stepped daintily into the pool. Or at least she *tried* to

do that, but it was deeper than she thought and she fell in right over her head. When she came up again,

- she *shook her head*
- she *pushed her hair back*
- and she *wiped her eyes*

Woman   Oh dear, silly me! Now I'll *have* to buy a new outfit.

Narrator   Later, Bart saw a man approaching, with a few friends.

Bart   He's got his own heavies. I wonder what's wrong with him: a bunion, perhaps, or a receding hairline?

Narrator   When the water rippled, the man stood still. Bart got angry.

Bart   Look, you may as well get on with it. At this rate neither of us is going to benefit.

Jesus   Are you waiting to get in the pool?

Bart   Well, actually I'm frying some chips. What does it look like? I'm sorry, but I'm getting really fed up. I've been lying here for ages, and every time the water ripples someone else gets there first.

Jesus   I'm not rushing to jump in.

Bart   Well, in that case could you help me?

Jesus   Why don't you just get up and pick up that bed of yours and go home?

Narrator   That did it! Bart was furious! Before he knew what he was doing, he was on his feet and wagging an accusing finger in the man's face. Then he caught on.

Bart   I'm standing up! For the first time in thirty-eight years.

Narrator   Before Bart could thank him, the mysterious healer had melted away into the crowd.

Bart   Well! Fancy helping someone and not waiting around to take the credit. What a kind man!

Narrator   But then, as you and I know, that's the kind of person Jesus is.

Back to the Good Old Days

Based on John 11:1-44

BEFORE THE DAY

Collect some of nature's signs of new life: buds from trees and bushes, little pot plants beginning to shoot. Decorate the front of the assembly hall with them.

• Think about the actions for all the children to join in during the story.

ON THE DAY

Introduction

We're going to think about new life, this morning. First, let's say our 'Thank you' Prayer.

'Thank you' Prayer

Thank you, God, for all you give us,
thank you for the earth and sea;
thank you, God, for special people,
thank you, God, for making me.

God's Story

Martha and Mary were friends of Jesus who lived with their brother Lazarus in a town called Bethany.

One day, while Martha was busy scrubbing the front step, Mary noticed that Lazarus was not very well. 'Oh, don't worry,' said Martha. 'I expect it's just a bit of a cold. Mind your feet – I've just cleaned that!'

Mary *was* worried, though. Lazarus was normally a very healthy person, and he wouldn't let a simple cold get him down, but just now he didn't seem to have the energy to do anything.

'I really think it's serious,' Mary persisted. 'He's even taken the day off from work.'

Martha was still scrubbing away at a stubborn mark that wouldn't come off. 'Oh, if you're really worried,' she said, 'you'd better get the doctor, but it won't be anything serious.'

The doctor soon arrived and examined Lazarus.

• He told him to *open his mouth*
• then he asked him to *say 'Ah'*
• then he asked him to *show him his tongue* (Ugh!)

The doctor wasn't very happy about things at all. 'He's caught a really dangerous infection,' he said, 'and I'm afraid you must be prepared for bad news. He's not going to get better.'

After the doctor had gone, Martha cried, 'If *he* can't save Lazarus, no one can. There isn't a better doctor in the area.'

'Yes there is! 'said Mary, suddenly brightening up. 'We can send for Jesus.'

'Jesus is a wonderful friend,' said Martha, 'but if a proper doctor can't help Lazarus I don't see what he can do. Still, I'm sure he'd want to know, so you'd better contact him. Lazarus can at least see him before he dies.'

When Jesus got Mary's note, he was very sad, and he sent a message back saying he would be there in a little while, and not to worry. Mary was surprised. 'Why doesn't he come straight away?' she wondered. Still, Mary had faith in Jesus. 'He's always right,' she said. 'Lazarus will be all right when Jesus gets here.' But he wasn't.

Next morning, Mary had a terrible shock when she went in to take Lazarus his early morning drink. Lazarus had died in the night, and Martha and Mary were both dreadfully upset. They hadn't expected it to happen so quickly.

'This is because of Jesus,' said Martha. 'I know he's a very busy man, but he should have come.'

'He's never been too busy for his friends, though,' said Mary. 'I just don't understand what's going on.'

Meanwhile, Jesus was still with his other friends, but he knew Lazarus had died. He decided it was time to go to Bethany. His disciples weren't very happy about that. 'Bethany's near Jerusalem,' they said, 'and the people there are out to get you. It's far too dangerous.'

Thomas persuaded the others to go, though. 'It might be dangerous,' he said, 'but Jesus is always there for us if we're in trouble. So if he's willing to risk going near Jerusalem, I'm with him.'

So they all set off. Martha heard Jesus was on his way and went to meet him. 'Wherever have you been?' she asked. 'If you'd been here, Lazarus wouldn't have died. Is this the thanks I get for all the cooking and cleaning I do for you?' Then she thought for a moment and said, 'I'm sorry, Jesus, I know that even now you can ask God for anything and he will give it to you.'

Jesus said, 'Your brother will live again, Martha. Do you believe that?'

'Oh, I believe we'll see him in heaven,' said Martha, 'but that's going to be a long wait.'

'Trust me,' said Jesus. 'New life is my business.'

'Mary will want to see you,' said Martha. 'You wait here and I'll get her.' Then she went back to the house and said to Mary, 'Jesus wants to see you. Come with me.'

Jesus saw Martha and Mary both crying, and he cried as well. 'Why didn't you come when I sent for you?' Mary asked him. 'I know you could have saved Lazarus.'

The friends who were comforting Martha and Mary felt the same way. 'Oh, great!' said one of them. 'Here's Jesus, four days too late. You'd have thought he could have got here in time and done something.'

'It's never too late for God,' said Jesus. 'And now you're going to see just how great God is.'

Jesus was as good as his word. He brought Lazarus back to life, to the amazement of the people around. Martha and Mary were overjoyed (and Lazarus was pretty pleased about it, too!) and their friends and neighbours learnt that they couldn't put limits on God's power. 'Isn't this wonderful!' said Mary. 'Now everything can be the way it used to be.'

'Yes,' said Jesus, 'back to the old life with all its joys and its sorrows. But stick with me, and you'll see something a lot more exciting than that.'

Now what on earth could he have meant?

Our Story

Point out the nature display. It's always terribly sad when someone dies, but renewal is built into creation. *We* don't see people come back from the dead the way Lazarus did, but we do believe that God has new life for them.

Prayers

We're Glad

Thank you, God,
for being cool, calm and collected.
Thank you for knowing what's best
and for doing things in your time,
not necessarily ours.

We're Sad

Please forgive us, God,
for not trusting you enough;
help us to be patient,
and to keep on trusting you
for however long we must.

Let's Pray for People

Loving God,
there are so many sad people:
sad because they're sick,
or because someone has died.
Please help them to know that you're in touch
even when it doesn't seem like it,
and to trust you to do what's best
when it's best to do it.

Songs

A butterfly, an Easter egg
Caterpillar, caterpillar
God sends a rainbow
I danced in the morning

Back to the Good Old Days!

God's Story

Narrator	Martha and Mary were friends of Jesus who lived with their brother Lazarus at Bethany. One day, Martha was just finishing scrubbing the front step.
Mary	Martha, I'm worried. Lazarus doesn't seem well.
Martha	Oh, he's OK. Careful – I've just cleaned that!
Mary	I really think it's serious. I'm calling the doctor.
Martha	Well make sure he wipes his feet when he arrives.
Doctor	I'm terribly sorry, but he's not going to get better.
Martha	Really, Mary! Why didn't you tell me about this before? *(To doctor)* You haven't tried hard enough! Get to work, and don't stop until you've cured him.
Mary	I know! Let's send for Jesus.
Narrator	Mary sent a message to Jesus. He sent back a note saying that he'd be along in a few days and not to worry.
Narrator	But Lazarus died before Jesus got there.
Martha	I know Jesus is busy, but he should have come.
Mary	He's never been too busy for his friends, though, Martha. I just don't understand what's going on.
Narrator	Meanwhile, Jesus knew Lazarus had died.
Jesus	It's time to go to Bethany.
Narrator	His disciples thought it was dangerous. Bethany was near Jerusalem. But Thomas persuaded them.
Thomas	It might be dangerous, but Jesus is always there for us if we're in trouble. I'm with him.
Narrator	Martha heard Jesus was on his way and went to meet him.
Martha	Wherever have you been? If you'd been here, Lazarus

wouldn't have died. Is this the thanks I get for all the cooking and cleaning I do for you? *(Pause)* I'm sorry, Jesus, I know that even now you can ask God for anything and he will give it to you.

Jesus Lazarus will live, Martha. Do you believe that?

Martha Oh, I believe we'll see him in heaven, but that's going to be a long wait.

Jesus Trust me. New life is my business.

Martha Mary will want to see you. I'll get her.

Mary Why didn't you come when I sent for you? I know you could have saved him.

Narrator When Jesus saw his friends crying, he cried as well. Then he went with them to the grave, which was a cave with a heavy stone in front of it.

Jesus Open the grave.

Martha What? After four days? Ugh!

Jesus Haven't you heard anything I've said to you? Open the grave and you'll see just how great God is.

Narrator So they rolled the stone away

Jesus Lazarus! Come out of there!

Narrator They heard scuffling sounds from inside the cave, and then Lazarus appeared at the entrance.

- He *blinked in the sun*,
- and he *yawned*
- then he gave a *big stretch*.

Jesus Why doesn't one of you stop staring and help him? Take that awful shroud off, for a start.

Mary Now everything can be the way it used to be.

Jesus Yes, back to the old life with all its joys and its sorrows. But stick with me, and you'll see something a lot more exciting than that.

A Donkey-load of Trouble

Based on John 12:12-19

BEFORE THE DAY

Get the children to draw or paint some pictures of really luxurious cars, and also some real 'old bangers', and put them up on the wall before the assembly.

• Think about the actions for all the children to join in during the story.

ON THE DAY

Introduction

According to the Bible, Jesus went into Jerusalem and was welcomed like a hero. We'll hear that story in a moment, but first we'll say our 'Thank you' Prayer.

'Thank you' Prayer

Thank you, God, for all you give us,
thank you for the earth and sea;
thank you, God, for special people,
thank you, God, for making me.

God's Story

I knew Jesus was trouble right from the time I first set eyes on him. He was at a dinner party, and some dreadful worthless woman came in and started kissing his feet. Then she went all weepy on him and tried to dry his feet with her hair. It was so embarrassing! 'Simon,' I said to myself, 'this man's a wrong 'un.' And I wasn't the only Pharisee who thought so, either. We all knew what a disgusting person that woman was, and more to the point we knew that Jesus knew it. So as soon as he let her touch him, and didn't tell her to pull herself together, that proved that he was no good either.

Now, you need to understand things from our point of view. It's because of us Pharisees that our religion hasn't died out long ago. We've had to stand up for what's right when other people have been saying that anything goes, and we're not going to let all we've worked for be thrown away now, by some namby pamby liberal who thinks saying 'God is love' means that absolutely anyone can be forgiven. What would the world be like if that got around! I mean, being terrified of God is the only thing that keeps some people in their place. So Jesus had to be stopped from giving sinners big ideas about getting forgiven. And we Pharisees were the ones to do it.

We were going to pick up a few of his friends and have them killed; hopefully, he'd get the message and shut up, and the people would lose interest in him. But before we could get started, Jesus made a kind of state visit to Jerusalem, and the custard pies really hit the fan, then.

It was near the time of the festival, and Jerusalem was filling up with visitors and tourists as usual. People get very excitable at this time, and it doesn't take much to start trouble. Well, I was just walking down the street minding my own business, when I heard someone shout, 'Hey! Jesus is coming,' and before you could say 'blasphemy' there was uproar: people running everywhere, ripping branches off the trees to wave like banners (no respect for the environment, these people) and generally getting hysterically undignified. I looked around and saw a chap called Saul, a young man training to be a lawyer. 'Hey, Saul,' I said. 'Over here.'

Saul came over. 'What's all the noise about?'

'Never mind that,' I hissed at him. 'Run to the temple, and tell the priests to put the guards on red alert and get down here at the double.'

At that point, I saw Jesus coming, and my blood froze. He was riding on a donkey! I knew then what he was up to. This was a secret sign, and I just hoped we weren't too late.

'Hurry!' I said to Saul. 'There's not a moment to lose. Oh, and for heaven's sake don't let anyone mention Zechariah's prophecy.'

He's a nice lad, Saul, but most of the time his head's in the clouds. I could tell he was only half with me, but I hoped it was the right half. He walked across the street before he stopped and stroked his beard. Well, I say 'beard': a few straggly hairs with nowhere to go, really. He turned round to face me, and I could see something was on his mind, but I couldn't get across the road in time to save the day.

- Saul *scratched his head*
- then he *stroked his beard* again
- then he *waved his hand* at me

'What was that about Zechariah's prophecy?'

I knew we were doomed. Immediately, the crowd started going even more wild. 'That's it!' Someone shouted. 'It's a sign. "Behold, your king comes to you riding on a donkey." Jesus is King! Jesus is King!'

It was a good thing that Saul was the other side of the road, or I'd have ended the day as a murderer. Saul saw the look on my face and disappeared into the crowd, which by now was growing by the second as people stampeded to meet Jesus. Then the shouts went up.

'Hosanna! Hosanna! Blessed is the one whom God has sent as our king!'

Everything was rapidly going pear shaped, and there was nothing I could do. All around me the crowd was jostling and shouting, and I knew if I tried to stop them I'd probably get torn limb from limb, they were so excited. All I could do was hope things didn't get any worse.

'I know him!' someone shouted. 'He's the one who raised Lazarus from the dead.'

'Pull the other one,' laughed someone else. 'It's got bells on.'

'No, it's true,' a third person shouted. 'I was there at the time.'

'So was I,' added another. 'Anyone who can raise the dead can have my vote.'

'Vote'? 'Vote'? Where did these people think they were: in a democracy or something? But it was no good fighting it; I'd have just got myself trampled underfoot. Not that I'm afraid of pain, mind you; it's the indignity.

Well, the whole thing turned into the most dreadful scene, with Jesus riding through on his donkey, people waving their branches, screaming 'Hosanna', and by the time Saul came back with the priests it was all totally out of hand. The High Priest, Caiaphas, was most upset. 'Are you mad?' he asked me. 'Did you really have to go and mention Zechariah's prophecy?'

That started them all off again, of course, and it took the rest of the day to get the people calm.

King Jesus, indeed! Something's definitely got to be done about him!

Our Story

Look at the pictures of cars and ask the children which ones really important people might arrive in. Jesus rode into Jerusalem as king, and his transport was the equivalent of an old banger!

Prayers

We're Glad

Loving God, we're so glad
that you love us
and want us to celebrate.
Thank you for showing us your love in Jesus,
who helped us see what real life
is all about.

We're Sad

We've all done it, God:
felt jealous of other people's happiness.
Please forgive us when we're petty,
and teach us to enjoy life
the way Jesus wants us to.

Let's Pray for People

Some people are so sad:
hung up on rules and regulations,
obsessed with their own dignity.
Please, God, set them free,
and help them to live!

Songs

Give me joy in my heart
Ho, ho, ho, hosanna
Hosanna, hosanna
We have a King who rides a donkey

A Donkey-load of Trouble

God's Story

Narrator I knew Jesus was trouble right from the time I first set eyes on him. We Pharisees have had to stand up for what's right when other people have been saying that anything goes, and we're not going to let all we've worked for be thrown away now, by some namby pamby liberal who thinks saying 'God is love' means that absolutely anyone can be forgiven. What would the world be like if that got around! I mean, being terrified of God is the only thing that keeps some people in their place. One day, Jesus made a kind of state visit to Jerusalem, and the custard pies really hit the fan, then.

It was near the time of the festival, and Jerusalem was filling up with visitors and tourists. I was just walking down the street minding my own business, when suddenly there was uproar: people running everywhere, ripping branches off the trees to wave like banners (no respect for the environment, these people) and generally getting hysterically undignified. I looked around and saw a young trainee lawyer called Saul.

Saul What's all the noise about?

Simon* Never mind that! Run to the temple, and tell the priests and the guards to get down here at the double.

Narrator At that point, I saw Jesus coming, and my blood froze. He was riding on a donkey! I knew then what he was up to. This was a secret sign, and I just hoped we weren't too late.

Simon Hurry! And for heaven's sake don't let anyone mention Zechariah's prophecy.

Narrator He's a nice lad, Saul, but most of the time his head's in the clouds. I could tell he was only half with me, but I hoped it was the right half. When he got across the road and turned round to face me, I could see something was on his mind, but I couldn't get to him in time to save the day.

* Simon and Narrator are the same person. As 'Simon' he engages in the dialogue with other characters; as 'Narrator' he addresses the audience.

- Saul *scratched his head*
- then he *stroked his beard* again
- then he *waved his hand* at me

Saul What was that about Zechariah's prophecy?

Narrator Immediately, the crowd started going even more wild.

Bystander 1 That's it! It's a sign. 'Behold, your king comes to you riding on a donkey.' Jesus is King! Jesus is King!

Narrator Saul saw the look on my face and disappeared into the crowd, which was now growing by the second as people stampeded to meet Jesus. Then the shouts went up.

Bystander 2 Hosanna! Hosanna! Blessed is the one whom God has sent as our king!

Narrator All around me the crowd was jostling and shouting, and I knew if I tried to stop them I'd probably get torn limb from limb, they were so excited.

Bystander 3 I know Jesus! He raised Lazarus from the dead.

Bystander 1 Pull the other one! It's got bells on.

Bystander 2 No, it's true. I was there at the time.

Bystander 4 Anyone who can raise the dead can have my vote.

Narrator 'Vote'? 'Vote'? Where did these people think they were; in a democracy or something? But it was no good fighting it; I'd have just got myself trampled underfoot. Not that I'm afraid of pain, mind you; it's the indignity. Well, by the time Saul came back with the priests it was all totally out of hand. The High Priest, Caiaphas was most upset.

Caiaphas Are you mad? Did you really have to go and mention Zechariah's prophecy?

Narrator That started them all off again, of course, and it took the rest of the day to get the people calm. King Jesus, indeed! Something's definitely got to be done about him!

The Lord of Smelly Feet

Based on John 13:3-15

BEFORE THE DAY

Arrange for a few volunteers from the children to have their hands washed by teachers in assembly.

- Think about the actions for all the children to join in during the story.

ON THE DAY

Introduction

Jesus was a very special kind of leader. Before we hear more about that, let's say our 'Thank you' Prayer.

'Thank you' Prayer

Thank you, God, for all you give us,
thank you for the earth and sea;
thank you, God, for special people,
thank you, God, for making me.

God's Story

Hello! Peter's the name. Well, it used to be Simon, but Jesus changed it; said something about my being a rock. I'm still not sure whether he meant me or my faith, but I've got my doubts whichever it was. I mean, I just don't seem to understand things the way I ought to.

Now, don't get me wrong. There's no one more loyal to Jesus than I am. In my better moments, I like to think I'd die for him if I had to. There again, there are other times (and don't breathe a word about this to anyone else) when I'm not so certain. Oh, sure, I put on a brave face in front of others. I've always been good at that. But deep down I'm often confused and sometimes just plain frightened. I suppose none of us really knows how we'd cope in a crisis until it happens. Still, as I said, I try to be loyal to Jesus.

And that's a lot more than I can say for some people. Take Judas, for example. I've had my doubts about that man from the start. *We* all know he's not to be trusted, but Jesus seems to be completely taken in by him. I'm sure he's not, really, but it does make you wonder when the man's got a reputation for dishonesty and Jesus makes him the group treasurer! And now, I'm quite convinced that Judas is up to no good. I've noticed him sneaking off when he thinks no one's looking, and then appearing back among us again hours later, as though he's never been away. I wouldn't mind, but there are some people who are out to get Jesus, and they always seem to know where he's going to be. Makes you think, doesn't it? And Jesus just goes on as normal; doesn't have any secrets; lets Judas in on all the plans. It doesn't make sense. That's why I have problems. Sometimes, I think Jesus is the special saviour of the world we've been promised, and other times he seems to be so foolish that I can't believe it.

He does strange things, too, for a leader. Like at that last supper we had together. We'd walked quite a long way and our feet were nothing special, I don't mind admitting – wouldn't have won any personal hygiene certificates, let's put it that way. I was really wishing we'd had a chance to freshen up before supper. Just as I was thinking that, Jesus got up and took his shirt off. Before we had a chance to ask what he was up to, he'd wrapped a towel round his waist and picked up a bowl and some soap. I wondered whether he'd spilt something and was going to wash himself, but he walked over to my brother and knelt down beside him. I didn't envy Jesus one little bit. Andrew might be family, but I have to be honest: when he's walked a few miles you don't want to get too close to his feet. By this time, everyone had stopped eating and was watching Jesus to see what he'd do. Very gently, he removed Andrew's sandals, and he was really nice.

- He didn't *pull a face*
- he didn't *hold his nose*
- and he didn't *turn his head away*

He just washed Andrew's feet and dried them

with the towel. It was really strange seeing Jesus kneeling down. Somehow, it would have been better for Andrew to kneel at Jesus' feet; after all, we do call Jesus 'Lord'.

Jesus didn't stop there. He went round everyone and did the same thing, until he came to me. I felt really awkward about it. Jesus is the boss, and washing people's feet is the job of a servant. I mean, *I* might wash *his* feet, but not the other way round. So I told him. 'If you think you're going to do that to me,' I said, 'then you can jolly well think again.'

Jesus looked hurt. 'Why?' he asked.

'Because it's not right!' was all I could find to say. 'Now put that silly bowl away and enjoy your meal.'

Jesus looked at me very patiently – the way he always does when I've just made a king-sized fool of myself. 'If I don't wash you,' he said quietly, 'you can't be the special friend I want you to be.'

I didn't understand, but I knew he meant it. 'Oh well,' I said, 'why didn't you say so before! In that case, you can wash my head as well – and what about my hands?'

'Don't go over the top, Peter,' replied Jesus. 'You've had a bath, haven't you? So it's just your feet need doing.'

I shut up after that, and Jesus finished off the job and sat down again. 'There,' he said. 'You call me "Lord", but I've just been your servant and washed your feet. Now if I can do that for you, surely you can do it for one another.'

I wasn't sure about that. Jesus is special – and you need to be, to get within two metres of Andrew's feet after a long walk. Jesus seemed to know what I was thinking.

'No servant's greater than the boss,' he said. 'And you call me the boss. So if I can do it, all of you can.'

Then I got it. All right, so it takes a while but I'm a better fisherman than I am philosopher. Jesus wanted us to serve one another. Things fell into place a bit then. I'd heard him saying things before about leaders acting as servants, but hadn't really taken it seriously. I'm on track now, though – got things really sussed. And I'm going to be the best, most loyal friend Jesus has, and I'll never misunderstand him or let him down again.

Well, all right, knowing me I probably will. But knowing Jesus, he'll forgive me, and help me to learn from it.

Our Story

Tell the children you're going to act out the story with some volunteers. Don't tell them straight away that it's only hands you'll be washing. Let them find that out for themselves when you start to do it. When each child has been washed, let them also wash the teachers' hands, so it's mutual. We care for each other.

Prayers

We're Glad

Thank you, Jesus,
for not being proud or snobbish.
Thank you for being our friend
and wanting only to do good things for us.

We're Sad

Are we like Peter, Jesus?
Do we put you on a pedestal so high up
that we can't hear you properly?
Please forgive us,
and be our friend.

Let's Pray for People

We pray for people who have power,
people who are called 'boss' or 'manager',
or other things like that.
Help them to be really *good* bosses
by serving the people in their charge.

Songs

A new commandment
The servant king
The world is full of smelly feet
We're going to shine like the sun

The Lord of Smelly Feet

God's Story

Narrator	Hello! Peter's the name. Well, it used to be Simon, but Jesus changed it; said something about my being a rock. I'm still not sure whether he meant me or my faith, but I've got my doubts whichever it was. I mean, I just don't seem to understand things the way I ought to. Now, don't get me wrong. There's no one more loyal to Jesus than I am. In my better moments, I like to think I'd die for him if I had to. There again, there are other times (and don't breathe a word about this to anyone else) when I'm not so certain. And Andrew agrees with me.
Andrew	D'you think Jesus knows what he's doing, Peter?
Peter*	Course he does. Why?
Andrew	Well, would you trust Judas with your money?
Peter	Not on your life.
Andrew	Jesus has made him the group's treasurer.
Narrator	That's the sort of thing I mean. Sometimes, I think Jesus is the special saviour of the world we've been promised, and other times he seems to be so foolish that I can't believe it. He does strange things, too, for a leader. Like at that last supper we had together. We'd walked quite a long way and my brother Andrew summed it all up.
Andrew	My feet are killing me.
Peter	Killing *you*! They're killing all of us. Most people's feet sweat, but yours should go professional.
Andrew	I can't help it.
Narrator	He'd got a point there. Anyway, when we were eating the supper, Jesus suddenly got up and took his shirt off. He walked over to my brother and knelt down beside him. Very gently, he removed Andrew's sandals, and he was really nice.

* Peter and Narrator are the same person. As 'Peter' he engages in the dialogue with other characters; as 'Narrator' he addresses the audience.

- He didn't *pull a face*
- he didn't *hold his nose*
- and he didn't *turn his head away*

He just washed Andrew's feet and dried them with the towel. Jesus didn't stop there. He went round everyone and did the same thing, until he came to me. I felt really awkward about it. Jesus is the boss, and washing people's feet is a servant's job. So I told him straight.

Peter   If you think you're going to wash my feet, think again.

Jesus   Why?

Peter   Because it's not right! You're the boss, not a servant.

Jesus   If I don't, you can't be the special friend I want you to be.

Peter   Oh well, why didn't you say so before! In that case, you can wash my head as well – and what about my hands?

Jesus   Don't go over the top, Peter. You've had a bath, haven't you? So it's just your feet need doing.

Narrator   I shut up after that. Jesus finished and sat down again.

Jesus   There. You call me 'Lord', but I've just been your servant and washed your feet. Now if I can do that for you, surely you can do it for one another.

Peter   That's different. You're special – and you need to be, to get within two metres of Andrew's feet after a long walk.

Jesus   No servant's greater than the boss, and you call me the boss. So if I can do it, all of you can.

Narrator   Then I got it. All right, so I'm a better fisherman than I am philosopher. Jesus wanted us to serve one another. I'd heard him saying things before about leaders acting as servants, but hadn't really taken it seriously. I'm on track now, though – got things really sussed. And I'm going to be the best, most loyal friend Jesus has, and I'll never misunderstand him or let him down again. Well, all right, knowing me I probably will. But knowing Jesus, he'll forgive me, and help me to learn from it.

Jesus Wins the Battle

Based on John 18:28-19:30

Get the children to write some headlines for the Jerusalem newspapers: 'INNOCENT MAN CRUCIFIED'; 'JESUS INNOCENT, SAYS MOTHER', etc. Write them in large bold letters, with some squiggles underneath to represent normal print. Post the 'cuttings' up on a board.

• Think about the actions for all the children to join in during the story.

ON THE DAY

Introduction

Soon, we'll be hearing the story of how people tried to hurt Jesus. First, we'll say our 'Thank you' Prayer.

'Thank you' Prayer

Thank you, God, for all you give us,
thank you for the earth and sea;
thank you, God, for special people,
thank you, God, for making me.

God's Story

Hello! My name's Caiaphas, and I'm the High Priest in Jerusalem. We'd been worried for a long time about this Jesus character, because he seemed like a trouble maker. Now let's be clear: he wasn't a priest, and he'd never been to theological college, but he did seem to know what he was talking about. And that sort are always dangerous. He went around telling people that God loves them even if they're not good. And he also told people who were not important – people like women and children, and disabled people – that they were as important as *we* were! Of course, we just couldn't allow it to go on. Once people like that start getting big ideas anything could happen – and then things might get nasty. So

we decided it would be best to get rid of him. That's why we arrested him and put him on trial.

Now the trouble was that he hadn't done anything wrong, so we had to twist things a bit – things he'd said that were really harmless, but we could make them sound worse than they were. Eventually, we managed to get him up for trial in front of the local Governor – a thoroughly untrustworthy politician called Pontius Pilate – and said Jesus was likely to start a revolution. Yes, all right, it was a long shot because we knew we couldn't make it stick, but we had another card up our sleeve. Pontius Pilate isn't a very good Governor. He's done some very silly things in the past few years, and given us excuses for starting riots – of course, we've always been careful to get other people to do the actual rioting so that *we* aren't caught. Anyway, all it would need would be one more truly awesome riot and he'd lose his job. So, while I reminded Pilate about that, and told him what a trouble-maker Jesus was, some of my priests were outside stirring up the crowd. Before he knew what had happened, Pilate had a group of very clever people in his palace telling him that if he knew what was good for him he'd kill Jesus; and at the same time he could hear the crowd outside getting more and more worked up.

Eventually, Pilate agreed to having Jesus crucified – nailed to a wooden cross until he died. I thought that would be the end of the matter. We'd get rid of Jesus, and at the same time we could convince the people that he'd been a fake all along. You see, Jesus was always preaching love and peace, and saying that you should turn the other cheek – all that kind of stuff – and I was looking forward to hearing him get angry – you know the sort of thing: shout and swear a bit, so that we could say he was all talk, and a hypocrite. Well, he talked all right, but you'll never guess what he said!

'Father, forgive them,' he said.

'They don't know what they're doing,' he said.

Here was this man, actually praying for forgiveness for us as the nails went in. I still can't get over it. There he was, hanging there in the heat, in horrible pain, and he really seemed to care more about others than himself. We tried everything to make him lose his cool.

- We *pulled faces*
- we *stuck out our tongues* (on second thoughts, put them back!)
- we even . . .*

But nothing worked. There were two rebels crucified, one on each side of him. One of them turned to him and asked for forgiveness. I was most upset, I can tell you – asking some perishing upstart for forgiveness when there were perfectly good priests there! Anyway, Jesus spoke really kindly to him. 'You'll be with me in paradise today,' he said. Rotten cheek if you ask me, but you've got to admire his courage. Then he looked down and saw his mother and a very special friend standing near the cross and started comforting them and telling them to look after each other. I tell you I don't understand it at all!

Then, when he actually died, he said the most amazing thing. 'It's complete,' he said, with real satisfaction in his voice, as though he'd achieved something. And I hate to admit it (and don't tell a soul I said this) but I think he had. After everything that had happened to him – all the people who had let him down or turned against him – he really did seem to love us all. I don't mind telling you I'm very upset by the whole thing. Why couldn't he just have yelled at us once? Why did he have to be so good all the time?

I was very worried by all this. I went away thinking that Jesus might be more trouble dead than alive. Now that *was* tempting Providence! You'll never guess what happened next. Just when I thought nothing could get any worse, the whole city started buzzing with rumours that he was alive again. It ruined everything. We'd just got rid of him, and got his friends nice and scared so they wouldn't cause any more trouble, and all of a sudden they were out there, full of confidence, telling everyone they met that Jesus was alive. And they really believed it! We couldn't frighten them any more. We tried threats, we tried blackmail – we even tried torture. No good. These people simply weren't afraid of us any longer.

Whatever we did to them, they just kept on celebrating because Jesus was alive!

I don't mind telling you it's got me really rattled. Still, I'm sure it'll all blow over in a few days . . .

Won't it?

Our Story

Look at the headlines. Because Jesus suffered injustice, and later rose from the dead, that means that he still cares about it. And whenever people are bullied, cheated, taunted, or wrongly punished, he feels it too. So how about we try to care just a little more?

Prayers

We're Glad

Thank you, God, for Jesus' victory.
Thank you for all the people
he has given courage,
to help them stand up for what is right.

We're Sad

We're sorry, Jesus, if ever
we've bullied people,
or taken advantage of them.
Help us to treat all other people
as if they were you.

Let's Pray for People

We pray for all who suffer for being good:
people who stand up against injustice,
and are accused of 'being political';
people who love others so much
that they get hurt badly themselves.
Please God, give them courage and hope.

Songs

From heaven you came
Jesus, remember me
There is a green hill
What kind of man was this

---

* Put thumbs to side of head and waggle fingers.

Jesus Wins the Battle

God's Story

Narrator Hello! My name's Caiaphas, and I'm the High Priest in Jerusalem. We'd been worried for a long time about this Jesus character. He said the most ridiculous things!

Jesus Of course God likes you to be good, but he won't stop loving you if you're not.

Narrator See what I mean? What sort of way is that to keep the rabble in their place?

Jesus And the people who are counted least important in this world are most important to God.

Narrator Now he's *really* gone too far! Once people like women and children and disabled people start getting big ideas, anything could happen. So we decided to get rid of him. Eventually, we managed to get him up for trial in front of the local Governor – Pontius Pilate.

Pilate What's the problem?

Caiaphas* He's going to start a rebellion.

Narrator All right, so it was a long shot, but we had another card to play. Some priests were outside stirring up the crowd.

Caiaphas Hear that? It's starting already.

Pilate Oh, no!

Caiaphas You've got to get rid of him. You know your boss isn't happy about all the recent riots. You don't want another.

Pilate All right, all right. I'll have him crucified.

Narrator I thought that would be the end of the matter. You see, Jesus was always preaching love and peace, and saying that you should turn the other cheek – all that kind of stuff – and I was sure we could make him shout and

* Caiaphas and Narrator are the same person. As 'Caiaphas' he engages in the dialogue with other characters; as 'Narrator' he addresses the audience.

swear a bit, so that we could say he was all talk, and a hypocrite. Well, you'll never guess what he said!

Jesus   Father, forgive them. They don't understand.

Narrator Here was this man, actually praying for forgiveness for us as the nails went in. I still can't get over it. There he was, hanging there in the heat, in horrible pain, and he really seemed to care more about others than himself. We tried everything to make him lose his cool.

- We *pulled faces*
- we *stuck out our tongues* (on second thoughts, put them back!)
- we even . . .*

But nothing worked. Then, when he actually died, he said the most amazing thing.

Jesus   It's complete. Everything is achieved.

Narrator I hate to admit it (and don't tell a soul I said this) but I think he *had* achieved something. After everything that had happened to him – all the people who had let him down or turned against him – he really did seem to love us all. I don't mind telling you I'm very upset by the whole thing. Why couldn't he just have yelled at us once? Why did he have to be so *good* all the time? I went away thinking that Jesus might be more trouble dead than alive. Now that *was* tempting Providence! You'll never guess what happened next. Just when I thought nothing could get any worse, the whole city started buzzing with rumours that he was alive again. It ruined everything. His friends were so full of it we couldn't frighten them any more. We tried threats, we tried blackmail – we even tried torture. No good. These people simply weren't afraid of us any longer. Whatever we did to them, they just kept on celebrating because Jesus was alive!

I don't mind telling you it's got me really rattled. Still, I'm sure it'll all blow over in a few days . . .

Won't it?

---

* Put thumbs to sides of head and waggle fingers.

About Turn!

Based on Acts 9:1-22

BEFORE THE DAY

Arrange for someone to dress up in a sinister costume, including mask or hood. Rehearse your act: The person is to creep up behind you during the assembly. If you ignore them, they will come up close behind and say 'Boo!' (at which you will be suitably startled), and then run off to return a few moments later. If you turn and face them, they are to freeze.

• Think about the actions for all the children to join in during the story.

ON THE DAY

Introduction

We're going to have a bit of a pantomime in a minute, but first we'll say our 'Thank you' Prayer.

'Thank you' Prayer

Thank you, God, for all you give us,
thank you for the earth and sea;
thank you, God, for special people,
thank you, God, for making me.

God's Story

This is the story of Saul, and it begins just after Jesus had gone to heaven. Jesus' disciples were going round all the country saying that Jesus was alive, and he was really the special person God had been promising to send, and lots of people were believing it and were becoming Christians.* Saul wasn't at all happy with that! He was a Pharisee, and they had thought they'd got rid of Jesus when he was crucified, but now here were his friends going round saying all these things! It seemed as though Jesus was stronger now than he ever had been!

Saul was so convinced that his was the only right religion, and everyone else was wrong,

that he just couldn't wait to start frightening Christians. He got people to spy on their friends; he sent agents out to listen at key-holes; he even got some people to pretend to be friends of Jesus, so that they could get into the meetings and give long lists of names to him afterwards. Before long, it simply wasn't safe to be a Christian at all, but the strange thing was that people still kept on joining up. They seemed to be so convinced that Jesus was God's Son that they were prepared to die if necessary. Saul couldn't understand it. How could they be so wrong, and so committed? Deep in his mind, where he was hardly aware of it himself, a tiny bit of doubt began to grow. So Saul did what people always do when that happens. He worked even harder, to try and pretend that the doubts weren't there. So he became really vicious, and went rampaging around chasing Christians and getting them killed. He was on the council, so after he'd caught them he would vote for the death penalty as well. He even tried to bully people into saying things they wouldn't have said. He was terrible! Then, one day, someone told him about a group of Christians at a town called Damascus. 'What!' he said. 'Surely it hasn't spread as far as that! We've got to stop it before it goes any further.' He makes it sound like a nasty disease, doesn't he? And in a way that's what he thought it was – and the people were the germs that had to be killed.

Saul asked for an appointment with the High Priest. 'This new religion has spread to Damascus,' he said. 'If we don't stop it, it will be all over the world.'

'It's very worrying, I agree,' said the High Priest. 'What will happen to people like us if this new religion takes over? We could end up just like ordinary people!' The High Priest shuddered at the very thought of being 'ordinary', and went on, 'What d'you think we should do?'

'Give me a warrant with your seal on it,' said Saul, 'and I'll take a few heavies with me and deal with them.'

The High Priest signed the warrant, and Saul went and got his mob together. Then they set off for Damascus. 'We'll show them who's really in charge of things!' he thought.

---

* According to scripture, the term 'Christians' had not yet been coined, but it is used here for the sake of simplicity.

Along the road they travelled, with Saul getting more and more excited all the time as he tried to quieten that dreadful little voice inside him by saying nasty things about Christians, and what he was going to do to them. Suddenly, a bright light flashed from the sky; a light so bright that it made the midday sun seem quite dim! Saul was terrified!

- He *covered his eyes*
- he *peeped through his fingers*
- and he quickly *covered his eyes* again

Then he heard a voice, and this time he couldn't drown it out or pretend that it wasn't there.

'Saul, Saul, why are you persecuting me? Why are you fighting so hard against that inner voice?'

Saul was terrified. 'Who are you?' he asked, although he was afraid he probably knew the answer.

'Don't give me that, Saul!' the voice answered. 'Deep down, you know who I am – you've been trying not to listen to me for months. I'm Jesus. I'm the one you're being so nasty to – because when you hurt my friends you hurt me, too.'

'What shall I do?' asked Saul.

'Get up and go to Damascus and join the Christians.'

So Saul got up, but he couldn't see anything, and had to be helped by his friends.

When they got to Damascus, Saul was met by a Christian called Ananias. 'I don't know what's going on,' said Ananias, 'but God seems to want me to meet you. I hope you're not going to kill me and my friends.'

Ananias wasn't the only one who was surprised. The religious leaders in Damascus had been waiting for Saul to get rid of the Christians for them. Imagine their surprise when they found he was one of them!

Our Story

Brief the children carefully, You've been told that there's a very strange person around, and if the children see them they are to tell you. Then begin talking generally about the story. When the figure appears behind you the children will shout, but you ignore them and eventually get a fright. Let this happen a few times before turning to confront the figure who freezes. Advance boldly, remove the hood and say, 'Why it's just our old friend, X!' Sometimes, the questions and doubts we have about things seem threatening, so like Saul we try to ignore them. But if we face them, we usually find they're really not dangerous at all.

Prayers

We're Glad

Thank you, God,
for giving us questioning minds.
Help us to listen to them,
and face the questions
so that our faith can grow.

We're Sad

We're sorry, God,
for trying to ignore you,
for wanting everything to be simple
and dull.
Please give us the courage to listen
to that little questioning voice.

Let's Pray for People

Please, God, help all people to trust you,
even when you seem to be raising
dangerous questions.

Songs

A still small voice
Father, I place into your hands
Make me a channel of your peace
One more step along the world I go

About Turn!

God's Story

Narrator This is the story of Saul, and it begins just after Jesus had gone to heaven. Jesus' disciples were going round all the country saying that Jesus was alive, and he was really the special person God had been promising to send, and lots of people were believing it and were becoming Christians.* Saul wasn't at all happy with that!

Saul We thought we'd got rid of Jesus, and now his friends are saying he's alive. Makes us look real fools!

Narrator Saul was so convinced that his was the only right religion, and everyone else was wrong, that he just couldn't wait to start frightening Christians. He got people to spy on their friends; he sent agents to listen at keyholes; he even got some people to go to the meetings pretending to be friends of Jesus, and give lists of names to him afterwards. Before long, it simply wasn't safe to be a Christian at all, but the strange thing was that people still kept on joining up. They seemed to be so convinced that Jesus was God's Son that they were prepared to die if necessary. Saul couldn't understand it.

Saul How can they be so wrong, and so committed? I *know* they're wrong. They *must* be wrong. There *can't* be any truth in it at all.

Narrator Deep in his mind, where he was hardly aware of it himself, a tiny bit of doubt began to grow. So Saul did what people always do. He worked even harder to try and pretend that the doubts weren't there. He went rampaging around getting Christians killed. Then, someone told him there were Christians at Damascus.

Saul What! Surely it hasn't spread as far as that! We've got to stop it before it goes any further.

Narrator Saul asked for an appointment with the High Priest.

---

* According to scripture, the term 'Christians' had not yet been coined, but it is used here for the sake of simplicity.

Saul This new religion has spread to Damascus. If we don't stop it, it will be all over the world.

High Priest It's very worrying, I agree. What will happen to people like us if this new religion takes over? We could end up just like ordinary people! Ugh! What d'you think we should do?

Saul Give me a warrant with your seal on it, and I'll take a few heavies with me and deal with them.

Narrator The High Priest signed the warrant, and Saul went and got his mob together. Then they set off for Damascus. Along the road they travelled, with Saul getting more and more excited all the time as he tried to quieten that dreadful little voice inside him by saying nasty things about Christians, and what he was going to do to them. Suddenly, a bright light flashed from the sky; a light so bright that it made the midday sun seem quite dim! Saul was terrified!

- He *covered his eyes*
- he *peeped through his fingers*
- and he quickly *covered his eyes* again

Jesus Saul, Saul, why are you persecuting me? Why are you fighting so hard against that inner voice?

Saul Who are you?

Jesus Don't give me that, Saul! Deep down, you know who I am – you've been trying not to listen to me for months. I'm Jesus. *I'm* the one you're being so nasty to, because when you hurt my friends you hurt me, too.

Saul What shall I do?

Jesus Get up and go to Damascus and join the Christians.

Narrator The religious leaders in Damascus had been waiting for Saul to get rid of the Christians for them. Imagine their surprise when they found he was one of them!

Peter the Miracle Worker

Based on Acts 9:31-35

BEFORE THE DAY

Set the children this exercise: without moving from their seats, they are to look around the room and try to take in as much detail as possible. What are the good things about the room? What things could be done to improve it? Draw up a list of suggestions and display it in the assembly area.

• Think about the actions for all the children to join in during the story.

ON THE DAY

Introduction

We're going to hear a lovely miracle story in a moment. First, we'll say our 'Thank you' Prayer.

'Thank you' Prayer

Thank you, God, for all you give us,
thank you for the earth and sea;
thank you, God, for special people,
thank you, God, for making me.

God's Story

Aeneas watched Rachel getting his dinner, and sighed, 'I bet you're sorry you married me, aren't you?'

'I do wish you wouldn't keep saying that!' Rachel replied. 'I don't regret anything at all.'

'But we used to do so much before I got ill,' Aeneas insisted. 'Remember those wonderful walking holidays in the hills, and how we used to dance the evenings away?'

Rachel smiled, happily. 'Yes, I do,' she said. 'I've got lots of wonderful memories, but most importantly of all I've got you.'

'Fat lot of good I am now,' moaned Aeneas. 'I can't even hold my own spoon – you have to do *everything* for me.'

'And you'd do it for me, if we were reversed,'

said Rachel crossly. 'Now stop feeling sorry for yourself or you'll be doing it on your own because I don't.' She came over with his dinner and started to help him eat it.

Rachel really wished that Aeneas could be well again; not for her own sake but for his. She knew that being active had always been important to him, and although she loved to care for him she longed to see him striding around as he used to. It was eight years since the illness had struck him, and no one had any idea what it was.

One day, Rachel heard that the famous Christian apostle, Peter, was in the area, and invited him to come and stay. Aeneas was very pleased, even though rather embarrassed. 'Peter's such a fit man,' he said. 'Just think of the miles he and Jesus walked together when Jesus was on earth. I hope he won't mind seeing me like this.'

Rachel was excited. 'Just think: someone who actually knew Jesus – shared meals with him, listened to him – it's almost too good to be true.'

When Peter arrived, he went straight in to see Aeneas. 'It's so good of you and Rachel to put me up,' he said. 'I hope you'll let me do something for you, as well.'

'That's very kind of you,' said Aeneas, 'but we do very well on the whole – although why Rachel puts up with all the work I make for her I'll never know.'

As they ate dinner, Peter said to Aeneas, 'If there were one thing you could wish for, what would it be?'

'I'd have thought that was obvious!' Aeneas answered.

'Maybe,' said Peter, 'but Jesus taught me never just to assume the obvious. So tell me what you'd most wish for.'

'To be able to hold the spoon for myself, and go outside after dinner to watch the sunset without having to be carried.'

Peter looked pleased. 'Now there's a funny thing,' he said. 'That's exactly what Jesus wants as well. So don't just lie there, get up and make your bed. And get a move on or you'll be too late for sunset.'

Aeneas thought at first that Peter was teasing him very cruelly. Then he began to feel a tingling sensation in his toes and fingers. He hadn't felt anything at all in them for eight years! Then he found himself doing strange things.

- He *wiggled his fingers*
- he *wiggled his toes*
- then he *clapped his hands together*

'Hey, what's going on!' he exclaimed. 'How did I get to be able to do this?'

They all laughed and hugged one another, and then Peter said, 'Hadn't we better go outside and see that sunset?' And somehow, they managed to stagger through the door together, still hugging each other, still laughing, and all the time thanking God for making it possible.

Peter thought that he might even be the happiest of the three of them, in a funny sort of way. 'I've always just taken it for granted that I could do all kinds of things,' he said. 'Now I realise just how important the little things in life are.'

Peter went early to bed that evening. He knew that Aeneas and Rachel would be out on the veranda for a long time. They had a lot to talk about; life was going to be very different for them both from now on.

'How about a holiday?' suggested Aeneas. 'We could go and visit all our old haunts and see if I can still remember how to do the Nazareth Two-step.'

'You won't have forgotten that,' Rachel assured him. 'You were always too good at it for that.'

'Great!' said Aeneas. 'As soon as you've done the washing-up we can start planning it.'

Rachel looked puzzled. 'Washing-up?' she asked. 'Why should *I* do the washing-up?'

Aeneas looked blank for a moment, and then his face broke into a big grin. 'You're right,' he said. '*Now* we can do it together.'

Our Story

Show the children the suggestion list the class drew up. Perhaps they could do the same for the assembly area. Emphasise that this was done just using their eyes, their brains and – most importantly – by working together. Although life's a lot easier if we can use our arms and legs, Aeneas shouldn't have thought himself useless just because he couldn't – should he?

Prayers

We're Glad

Thank you, God,
for all that we can do.
And thank you for other people
who help us with what we find difficult.

We're Sad

Sometimes we label people as 'disabled'
and then ignore all their abilities!
Please help us to concentrate
on what people can do
more than what they can't.

Let's Pray for People

Please God, bless all people
who are frustrated by life,
because the things we think are so ordinary
are difficult for them.
And bless all the people who care for others.
Show us what we can do to make life better.

Songs

He gave me eyes so I could see
He's got the whole world in his hand
Jesus put this song into our hearts
Thank you for the summer morning

Peter the Miracle Worker

God's Story

Narrator	Aeneas watched Rachel getting his dinner, and sighed.
Aeneas	I bet you're sorry you married me, aren't you?
Rachel	I do wish you wouldn't keep saying that!
Aeneas	But we used to do so much before I got ill. Remember those wonderful walking holidays in the hills, and how we used to dance the evenings away?
Rachel	Yes, I do. I've got lots of wonderful memories, but most importantly of all I've got you.
Aeneas	Fat lot of good I am now. I can't even hold my own spoon – you have to do *everything* for me.
Rachel	And you'd do it for me. Now stop feeling sorry for yourself or you'll be doing it alone because I don't.
Narrator	Rachel really wished that Aeneas could be well again; not for her own sake but for his. She knew that being active had always been important to him. One day, Rachel heard that the famous Christian apostle Peter was in the area, and invited him to come and stay. Aeneas and Rachel were very pleased.
Rachel	Just think: someone who actually knew Jesus – shared meals with him, listened to him – it's almost too good to be true.
Narrator	When Peter arrived, they all sat down together to a meal.
Peter	It's so good of you and Rachel to put me up. I hope you'll let me do something for you, as well, Aeneas.
Aeneas	That's very kind of you, but we do very well on the whole – although why Rachel puts up with all the work I make for her I'll never know.
Peter	If you could wish for one thing, what would it be?

Aeneas   I'd have thought that was obvious!

Peter   Maybe, but Jesus taught me never just to assume the obvious. So tell me what you'd most wish for.

Aeneas   To be able to hold the spoon for myself, and go outside after dinner to watch the sunset without having to be carried.

Peter   Now there's a funny thing! That's exactly what Jesus wants as well. So don't just lie there, get up and make your bed. And get a move on or you'll be too late for sunset.

Narrator   Aeneas thought at first that Peter was teasing him very cruelly. Then he began to feel a tingling sensation in his toes and fingers. He hadn't felt anything at all in them for eight years! Then he found himself doing strange things.

- He *wiggled his fingers*
- he *wiggled his toes*
- then he *clapped his hands together*

Aeneas   Hey, what's going on! How come I can do this?

Peter   Hadn't we better go outside and see that sunset?

Narrator   Somehow, they managed to stagger through the door together, hugging each other, laughing, and all the time thanking God for making it possible. Aeneas and Rachel stayed up late that night, talking.

Aeneas   How about a holiday? We could go and visit all our old haunts and see if I can still remember how to do the Nazareth Two-step.

Rachel   You won't have forgotten that. You were always too good at it for that.

Aeneas   Great! As soon as you've done the washing-up we can start planning it.

Rachel   Washing-up? Why should *I* do the washing-up?

Aeneas   You're right! *Now* we can do it together.

Paul Starts a Riot

Based on Acts 21:27-23:11

BEFORE THE DAY

Collect some examples (colour photographs from magazines would do) of distinctive art and craft work from other cultures. Then consider the beliefs we have in common, e.g.: sanctity of life, love, family values, community, etc. Make an interesting display, interspersing the 'shared' with the 'different'.

- Think about the actions for all the children to join in during the story.

ON THE DAY

Introduction

In a moment, we'll be hearing a story about some silly, prejudiced people. First, we'll say our 'Thank you' Prayer.

'Thank you' Prayer.

Thank you, God, for all you give us,
thank you for the earth and sea,
thank you, God, for special people,
thank you, God, for making me.

God's Story

Paul was in the temple in Jerusalem. He'd come back after a tour of other countries as a missionary. Everywhere he went he had told people about Jesus, and some had liked what he had said, but others hadn't – so he'd made a lot of enemies as well as friends.

As it happened, one of the enemies he'd made was also in Jerusalem. Now if he'd been on his own, Reuben wouldn't have said 'Boo!' to a turtle dove, but he felt safe in a crowd. So he started shouting.

'Ooh! Look at that man!' he cried. 'That's Paul, that is! He's the one that spreads false religion everywhere. He's been telling people all kinds of dangerous things – but worst of all, he's brought nasty pagan forriners into this temple!'

That did it! People like Reuben are not really concerned about truth, but you can always get them wound up by talking about 'pagans' and 'forriners'. So before long, there was a full-scale riot going on. Reuben was loving it, because he didn't realise how silly he looked!

- He would *point his finger*
- he would *shake his fist*
- he would *wave both fists in the air*

Some of Reuben's friends dragged Paul outside the temple – much to the relief of the priests who immediately locked the doors to protect themselves. Just in the nick of time, a massive squad of soldiers arrived.

'All right – what's this all about?' the commander asked. Everyone started talking at once, and he couldn't make any sense of what they were saying; so he had Paul put in handcuffs and led him away. Reuben was really pleased. 'Well done, Officer,' he called out. 'I knew we could always rely on the Romans to keep nasty people like him under control.' It didn't seem to occur to Reuben that the Romans were 'forriners', and he was supposed to hate them!

As they were about to take Paul into the prison, he asked the commander, 'Can I say a few words to the crowd, please?'

The commander agreed, and he got his soldiers to quieten everybody down. Paul told the people all about how much he used to hate Christianity, and how he was converted. The crowd listened remarkably quietly, until he said something they *really* didn't like. 'God sent me,' he said, 'to tell people of other races about Jesus.'

'Forriners!' screeched Reuben, hysterically. 'What did I tell you? Forriners! Nasty little pagan forriners! Hordes of 'em!' And suddenly the crowd went absolutely wild again, demanding that Paul should be killed!

'Quick!' said the commander. 'Get him inside before they tear him apart! Take him down to the cells and flog him until he talks. I want to know what this is *really* all about.'

So the soldiers took Paul downstairs, and began to tie him up ready to be flogged, but Paul had a surprise in store.

'Tell me,' he asked, in a very reasonable tone of voice. 'Are you allowed to flog a Roman citizen without a trial? I mean, I'd hate you nice people to get into any trouble.'

'You?' scoffed the commander. 'A Roman citizen? It cost me a lot of money to become one of those.'

'That's your problem,' Paul answered. 'I was born one.'

Suddenly, all the soldiers started being very nice to Paul.

'Let me help you out of those nasty ropes.'

'You can borrow my cloak to keep you warm.'

'Would you like a nice glass of wine, *Sir*?'

And the commander said, 'Er, we don't need to let this little misunderstanding go any further, do we, Sir?'

Next day the commander sent for the religious people to try and sort things out.

Paul spoke to them, and they listened fairly politely – apart from the occasional punch in the face which was quite standard stuff for them – until Paul started talking about resurrection.

'Oh, not that nonsense!' said one of the priests.

'Don't start that again,' shouted a Pharisee. 'If you priests were doing your job, *everyone* would believe in resurrection.'

'Rubbish!' shouted another priest. 'Go and learn some theology before you open your big mouth.'

'We were wrong about Paul,' another Pharisee called out. 'Anyone who believes in resurrection can't be all bad.'

'Oh, go and polish your lucky horseshoe,' yelled a priest. 'Superstitious claptrap!'

The commander turned to Paul, and said, 'I'm going to lock you up again, for your own protection. If that mob get their hands on you you'll be dog food. Why *do* religious people hate each other so much?'

With that, he took Paul away to a room in the barracks and his soldiers dispersed the rabble.

That night, Paul had a dream in which Jesus spoke to him. 'Don't worry, Paul,' he said. 'You've done well in telling people about me here. Now you'd better start polishing up your Latin so you can tell them about me in Rome.'

And that is a whole story in itself.

Our Story

Point out the display. People like Reuben miss so much by thinking no one else has anything good to offer. And anyway, he was ignoring all the really important things that we share!

Prayers

We're Glad

Thank you, God,
for being so mysterious;
for not being so small
that we can understand you!
Even though we've got for ever to get to know
   you,
we're never likely to get bored!

We're Sad

We're sorry, God,
for the times we think we're right
and everyone else is wrong.
Teach us to listen more carefully
to what other people have learnt about you.

Let's Pray for People

We pray for all people of faith,
that we may learn to value variety.
Help us to understand that mystery
is part of what makes you 'God'!

Songs

All creatures of our God and King
Be still, for the presence of the Lord
In the first stage of seeking
There are hundreds of sparrows

Paul Starts a Riot

God's Story

Narrator	Paul was in the temple in Jerusalem. So was one of his enemies. Now if he'd been alone, Reuben wouldn't have said 'Boo!' to a turtle dove, but he felt safe in a crowd.
Reuben	Ooh! Look at that man! That's Paul, that is! He's the one that spreads false religion everywhere. And worst of all, he's brought nasty pagan forriners into this temple!
Narrator	That did it! People like Reuben don't care about truth, only about 'pagans' and 'forriners'. There was soon a riot going on. Reuben didn't realise how silly he looked!

- He would *point his finger*
- he would *shake his fist*
- he would *wave both fists in the air*

Some of Reuben's friends dragged Paul outside the temple – much to the relief of the priests who immediately locked the doors to protect themselves. Just in the nick of time, a massive squad of soldiers arrived.

Commander	All right – what's this all about?
Narrator	Everyone started talking at once, and he couldn't make any sense of what they were saying; so he had Paul put in handcuffs and led him away. Reuben was thrilled!
Reuben	Well done, Officer. I knew we could always rely on the Romans to keep nasty people like him under control.
Narrator	It didn't seem to occur to Reuben that the Romans were 'forriners', and he was supposed to hate them!
Paul	Can I say a few words to the crowd, please?
Commander	I suppose so. Shut up and listen, you lot.
Narrator	Paul told the people all about how he was converted to Christianity. The crowd listened remarkably quietly, until he said something they *really* didn't like.
Paul	God sent me to tell people of other races about Jesus.

Reuben	What did I tell you? Nasty little pagan forriners!
Commander	Quick! Take Paul to the cells and flog him until he talks. I want to know what this is *really* all about.
Narrator	So the soldiers took Paul downstairs, and began to tie him up, but Paul had a surprise in store.
Paul	Are you allowed to flog a Roman citizen without a trial? I mean, I'd hate you nice people to get into any trouble.
Commander	You? A Roman citizen?
Paul	You'd better believe it.
Commander	Let me help you out of those nasty ropes.
Soldier	Would you like a nice glass of wine, *Sir*?
Commander	Er, we don't need to let this little misunderstanding go any further, do we, Sir?
Narrator	Next day the commander sent for the religious people to try and sort things out. They were quite polite to Paul – apart from the occasional punch in the face which was quite standard stuff – until Paul mentioned resurrection.
Priest 1	Oh, not that nonsense!
Pharisee 1	If you priests did your job, *everyone* would believe in it.
Priest 2	Rubbish! Go and learn some theology.
Pharisee 2	We were wrong about Paul. Anyone who believes in resurrection can't be all bad.
Priest 1	Oh, go and polish your horseshoe. Superstitious claptrap!
Commander	I'm locking you up again, for your protection. Why *do* religious people hate each other so much?
Narrator	With that, he took Paul away to a room in the barracks and his soldiers dispersed the rabble. That night, Paul had a dream in which Jesus spoke to him and told him to polish up his Latin. He was going to take the gospel to Rome! And that is a whole story in itself.

'Let's Get Paul!'

Based on Acts 23:12-25:12

BEFORE THE DAY

Ask the children whether they have ever thought things were going really badly wrong, only to have something unexpected happen which turned out for good. In the unlikely event of a total silence, have one of your own ready. Ask the children to draw or paint something to illustrate the story, and put the pictures on display.

• Think about the actions for all the children to join in during the story.

ON THE DAY

Introduction

Sometimes – not always, but sometimes – when everything seems to be going wrong, something good comes out of it. We're going to learn about hope in a moment, but first we'll say our 'Thank you' Prayer.

'Thank you' Prayer.

Thank you, God, for all you give us,
thank you for the earth and sea;
thank you, God, for special people,
thank you, God, for making me.

God's Story

Paul was in prison – not because he had done anything wrong but to protect him from a group of prejudiced people who were out to get him.

'We'll have to kill him ourselves,' said Reuben. 'Just because Paul's a Roman citizen, that lot are too frightened to do anything.'

'I know,' said another man, called Sim. 'We could go in under cover of darkness, scale the wall holding knives in our teeth, overpower the guards, steal their keys, fight our way through to the dungeons and kill him there.'

'You've been reading those *Special Action Superheroes* stories again, haven't you?' said Reuben, sadly.

'I know,' said another person. 'Why don't we get the chief priests to ask the commander to bring Paul to them for an opinion, and then ambush him before he gets there? They wouldn't send much of a guard with him, and the forty of us could soon deal with them.'

But what they didn't know was that Paul's nephew had overheard them, and he went to warn the commander.

Reuben and his forty fearsome friends were lying in wait for Paul when they heard the sound of horses and soldiers approaching. 'Great jumping Jehoshaphat!' said Reuben. 'How many of them are there?' Instead of the half-dozen guards they'd expected, there were nearly five hundred – and armed to the teeth.

'No problem,' said Sim. 'We could sneak up on them stealthily like cats, holding our daggers in our teeth, and pick them off one by one from the back. That's what the *Special Action Superheroes* would do.'

'Oh, go and finish reading your comic!' said Reuben. 'Come on, everyone.'

So they went home, and Sim told his wife how he'd fought fifty Roman soldiers single-handed. As he told the story,

• he *waved an imaginary sword*
• he *sheathed his imaginary sword*,
• and he *cut his imaginary finger*. Ouch!

'Very nice, dear,' said his wife. 'Would you like a nice drink of hot milk?'

The soldiers took Paul all the way to the town of Caesarea, to the Governor's house, and the chief priests had to go there and explain what it was about Paul they didn't like.

'Paul's a nuisance,' explained Ananias, the High Priest. 'He's been spreading his outrageous religious ideas around – not to mention bringing people we don't like into the temple. He's a perfect pest!'

'Really!' mused the Governor, whose name was Felix. 'And I thought that according to your religion no one was perfect! Well, I can't go killing everybody whom you don't like, there'd be very few people left at all. Tell you what, give me a few days to think about it.'

After they had gone, he said to Paul, 'Sorry about this. I could just let you go, but then there's all the paperwork, and the legal fees – it's a *very* expensive business.'

'If you're asking for a bribe . . .' said Paul.

'Oh dear me, no!' exclaimed Felix. 'But of course a contribution to the expenses just might speed things up a bit.'

'Don't worry,' said Paul. 'I'll wait.'

Felix kept Paul waiting for two years hoping that Paul would bribe him to let him go, but Paul was just biding his time. After all, God had said he was to go to Rome, and God kept his promises. After those two years, a new governor took over from Felix. Festus was his name – and he was anxious to make a good impression with the religious leaders because he knew how troublesome they could be if he didn't. So he went to Jerusalem, and asked the priests if there was anything he could do for them.

'Yes,' said Ananias. 'You can kill Paul.'

'Why?' asked Festus. 'What's he done?'

'You'll think of something,' said Ananias. 'Just get rid of him.'

But Festus knew Paul was a Roman citizen, and that meant he had rights. So he arranged a show trial, with the chief priests there to give their evidence. But they hadn't got any. All they could really say was that they didn't like Paul. Festus would have let him go if he hadn't been trying to make a good impression on the priests. Then he had an idea.

'Look,' he said to Paul, 'all this religious stuff is nothing to do with us Romans. Why don't you just go along with these fellows and sort it out between yourselves?'

'You must think I came down in the last shower!' exclaimed Paul. 'Go along with them? Not on your life! If you won't listen to me, I'd better go to someone who will. I'm a Roman citizen and I have the right to be tried by the Emperor himself in Rome. So I appeal to him.'

'You don't appeal to *me* in the slightest!' thought Festus, but he knew better than to say it. 'Well,' he said, 'if that's what you want, that's what will happen. You'll go to Rome.'

That got Paul out of reach of the priests, and it also did something else. It gave him a chance to spread the story of Jesus even further – which was precisely what they had been trying to stop him doing.

God really does work in very mysterious ways!

Our Story

Point out the pictures, and tell the story. Have the children present got other stories they can tell? Of course, things don't always work out as neatly as this, and of course Paul had to suffer for an awfully long time. But at least it means we needn't lose hope.

Prayers

We're Glad

Thank you, God,
for being involved in our world.
Thank you for sticking with us
through the hard times,
and giving us hope.

We're Sad

Sometimes, it's not easy to see
what you're about, God!
So we lose sight of you
and think we're all alone.
Forgive us for not trusting you enough.

Let's Pray for People

We pray for people
who are trapped as Paul was
between people who are out for trouble
and others who could help,
but only want a quiet life.
Please God, give us faith
to get involved,
and to show that you are at work.

Songs

Give me joy in my heart
I will enter his gates
Morning has broken
We're going to shine like the sun

'Let's Get Paul!'

God's Story

Narrator	Paul was in prison to protect him from Reuben and his horrible gang, who were out to get him.
Reuben	It's no good, we'll have to kill him ourselves.
Sim	I know. We could go in under cover of darkness, scale the wall holding knives in our teeth, overpower the guards, fight our way to the dungeons and kill him there.
Reuben	You've been reading those *Special Action Superheroes* stories again, haven't you, Sim? No, we'll get the chief priests to ask the commander to bring Paul to them for an opinion, and then ambush him before he gets there.
Narrator	But what they didn't know was that Paul's nephew had overheard them, and he went to warn the commander. So, when Reuben and his forty fearsome friends were lying in wait for Paul they had an unpleasant surprise.
Reuben	There must be five hundred guards around him!
Sim	No problem. Let's sneak up on them, holding our daggers in our teeth, and pick them off one by one from behind – like the *Special Action Superheroes* would do.
Reuben	Oh, go and read your comic! Come on, everyone.
Narrator	So they went home. Sim told his wife how he'd fought fifty Roman soldiers single-handed. As he told the story,

- he *waved an imaginary sword*
- he *sheathed his imaginary sword,*
- and he *cut his imaginary finger.* Ouch!

Wife	Very nice, dear. Would you like a nice drink of hot milk?
Narrator	The soldiers took Paul to Cesarea and to the Governor's house, and Ananias, the chief priest had to go and explain why he hated him.
Ananias	Paul spreads outrageous ideas, and brings people we don't like into the temple. He's a perfect pest, Felix!

Felix	And I thought that according to your religion no one was perfect! Well, if I killed everybody you don't like, there'd be very few left. Tell you what, let me think about it.
Narrator	Ananias left. Felix turned to Paul.
Felix	Sorry about this. I could let you go, but then there's all the paperwork, and the legal fees – it's *very* expensive.
Paul	If you're asking for a bribe . . .
Felix	Oh dear, no, but a contribution to expenses, perhaps . . .
Paul	Don't worry. I'll wait.
Narrator	Felix kept Paul waiting for two years hoping that Paul would bribe him to let him go. Then a new governor, Festus, took over from Felix. He was anxious to make a good impression, so he went to Jerusalem, and asked the priests if there was anything he could do for them.
Ananias	Yes, you can kill Paul.
Festus	Why? What crime has he committed?
Ananias	You'll think of something. Just get rid of him.
Narrator	A little later, Festus had an idea.
Festus	Look, Paul, all this religious stuff is nothing to do with us Romans. Why don't you just go along with these fellows and sort it out between yourselves?
Paul	You must think I came down in the last shower! If you won't listen to me, I'd better go to someone who will. I'm a Roman citizen and I have the right to be tried by the Emperor himself in Rome. So I appeal to him.
Festus	*(Aside)* You don't appeal to *me* in the slightest! *(To Paul)* Well, if that's what you want, you'll go to Rome.
Narrator	That got Paul out of reach of the priests, and it also did something else. It gave him a chance to spread the story of Jesus even further – which was precisely what they had been trying to stop him doing. God really does work in very mysterious ways!